SAY IT SAFELY

Legal Limits in Publishing, Radio, and Television

Say It Safely

LEGAL LIMITS IN PUBLISHING, RADIO, AND TELEVISION

By Paul P. Ashley

OF THE SEATTLE BAR

FOURTH EDITION

UNIVERSITY OF WASHINGTON PRESS · 1972

SEATTLE AND LONDON

The first edition of SAY IT SAFELY, published in 1956, replaced the author's ESSENTIALS OF LIBEL: A HANDBOOK FOR JOURNALISTS, published in 1948.

Second edition, revised, 1959
Third edition, revised, 1966
Fourth edition, revised, 1969
Second printing, 1970
Third printing, 1972

We have in this Country but one security. You may think that the Constitution is your security—it is nothing but a piece of paper. You may think that the statutes are your security—they are nothing but words in a book. You may think that an elaborate mechanism of government is your security—it is nothing at all, unless you have sound and uncorrupted public opinion to give life to your Constitution, *to give vitality to your statutes, to make efficient your government machinery.*

CHARLES EVANS HUGHES

PREFACE

> My dear, dear lord
> The purest treasure mortal times afford
> Is spotless reputation; that away,
> Men are but gilded loam or painted clay.
>
> King Richard II
> Act 1, Scene 1

This manual is a working tool designed for day-to-day use by all who write or process copy or speak over the air waves. It is not a reference work that should repose in the library or morgue, or on the shelf across the room.

Ten years of using *Say It Safely* (plus eight for its forerunner, *Essentials of Libel*) have demonstrated to thousands of craftsmen and executives the advantage of placing such a book on each desk, convenient to reach and use.

Since publication of the second edition in 1959 there have been significant changes—almost all to the good—in the law of qualified privilege. Whole chapters of that edition are, I am glad to say, outmoded. It became imperative that the book include a new and enlarged treatment of the situation—partly legal, partly practical—in respect to the coverage of crimes and criminal trials. So, while a few chapters remain virtually unchanged, it is correct to say that in practical application the third edition is a new book.

An effort has been made to bring in adequate new material covering radio, television, and photography, with special emphasis on the problems of the political broadcast and on-the-spot radio and television reports. As before, in addition to offering a condensed presentation of the law of libel, the manual discusses contempt of court and the developing concept of right of privacy.

Say It Safely is designed for personnel of newspapers, publishers of magazines and books, radio and television broadcasters, the wire services and broadcasting networks, advertising agencies, and students looking toward a career in the field of mass communication. It will also answer practical questions for the public relations counsel of corporations, government, and professional and trade associations.

In the preface to earlier editions I made grateful acknowledgment to lawyer friends throughout the country who read drafts of chapters or otherwise helped me avoid error. Similar acknowledgment was and is made to veteran journalists and to teachers who also read copy and made helpful suggestions. The number has multiplied. If I begin listing names, there will be no proper place to stop. A most hearty thanks to all of them.

There must be five exceptions. Chief Justice Hugh J. Rosellini of the Supreme Court of Washington, and Judge Eugene A. Wright of the superior court, both took time to review "Free Speech—Fair Trial" and related chapters. Their experience on the bench has been augmented by studies of the fundamentals for reaching balanced procedures—fair to litigants yet preserving freedom in reporting news. Richard H. Riddell of the Seattle Bar made suggestions in respect to the treatment of radio and television and political broadcasts; his comments were backed by his firsthand experience as counsel for stations. Paul Conrad, executive secretary of Allied Daily Newspapers of Washington, checked the entire manuscript from the viewpoint of some of those for whom it was primarily written. My partner, Daniel J. Riviera, reviewed the handling of the evolving rules in respect to qualified privilege and fair comment, and made helpful suggestions.

All who have helped me are exonerated from blame. Responsibility for sins of omission and commission are mine. It has been a pleasure to receive the hundreds of reports from those who have used the book professionally in their daily work and to know that students have been assisted by the funds it generates.

To further brevity and simplicity, citations to the authorities have been omitted. Though leaning heavily on the Restatement of the Law of Torts by the American Law Institute, I have not followed it in all respects.

Fourth Edition, 1969

Since publication of the third edition in 1966 readers have suggested that a discussion of violations of copyright and literary property should be included. So it has been—Chapter 18. The development of the rule of the *New York Times* case has been changed from prophecy to reality—principally pages 66 and 67. Otherwise there have been no significant changes from the third edition.

P.P.A.

NOTE: This book is published in cooperation with the Allied Daily Newspapers of Washington and the School of Communications, University of Washington. As in the past, all author's royalties will go to a scholarship fund for the School of Communications, University of Washington.

CONTENTS

1. The Arena   3
2. What Is Libel?   10
3. Keep Away from Libel Per Se   18
4. Intention and Mistake   28
5. Quotations and Ads   36
6. Privilege—Who Has It?   43
7. Qualified Privilege—Practical Application   50
8. Comment and Criticism   76
9. Truth, Consent, and Replies   86
10. Corrections and Retractions   90
11. Contempts of Court   93
12. Pictures—Still and Moving   99
13. Right of Privacy   107
14. Radio and Television   116
15. Political Broadcasts   122
16. Free Speech—Fair Trial   133
17. Danger Zones   151
18. Copyrights and Literary Property   160
19. Thirty   173
    Index   177

SAY IT SAFELY

Legal Limits in Publishing, Radio, and Television

CHAPTER 1

THE ARENA

We should never so entirely avoid danger as to appear irresolute and cowardly. But, at the same time, we should avoid unnecessarily exposing ourselves to danger, than which nothing can be more foolish.

CICERO

LIBEL may be defined as any false statement, written or broadcast, which tends to (i) bring a person into public hatred, contempt, or ridicule; (ii) cause him to be shunned or avoided; or (iii) injure him in his business or occupation.

Not all libelous statements can be forbidden. Many must, should, or may be made. A witness must be free to speak the truth as he remembers it, though his memory may be frail and he falsely brings disgrace upon his neighbor. A judge must announce the facts he finds have been proved, though he, too, may err. The lawmaker must be able to debate freely; what he says must be in the public domain, uncensored and unchanged. Governmental affairs must be under the searching light of criticism.

There is a continual contest within the law. Should communication of news and opinion be compressed into channels not harmful to individuals? Or should it be broadened for the public good? One aspect of the law of libel must protect persons. Another approach must recognize the people's right to know what goes on and to speak up in respect to public affairs. An equilibrium has not yet been reached.

I. History of Libel

Libel is not new in the law. The Papyrus of Hunefer shows the soul of that dignitary, then lately departed, pleading before the sun god, Osiris:

> I have not robbed;
> I have not slandered

and so on until he had pleaded not guilty to each of the forty-two offenses of which early Egyptian law took cognizance.

Moses commanded: "Neither shalt thou bear false witness against thy neighbor." The Far East punished slander. The Twelve Tables of Rome recognized defamation. Early Anglo-Saxon and Germanic laws took a serious view of insult by word or gesture. Punishments included excision of the tongue.

In England, a book on libel was written three hundred years ago. Under a French ordinance of the past century the publication of a libel was punished by whipping and, on a second offense, with death.

Lady Mary Wortley Montague remarked: "I am charmed with many points of the Turkish law. The proved authors of any notorious falsehood are burned on the forehead with a hot iron." If a South Pacific Islander hurts another person's body or his name, the *nanmarki*, the chief, must decide between them.

For a long time defamation has been universally recognized as a crime or as a civil wrong or as both. Redress for injury to reputation is one of the most cherished legal rights.

The rise of large newspapers during the nineteenth century brought special legal problems. Their capacity to inflict injury is enormous. But the daily deadlines make it difficult for the editor to take the precautions available to the publisher of a book or the writer of a speech. The current phenomenal growth of radio and television poses new problems. A nationwide (occasionally, it may be said, world-wide) broadcast reaches millions of people. Injury may be done in many states. Should the law permit a dozen suits based on the same broadcast?

Despite its long history, the law of libel is still in a period of evaluation. It reflects a continuing attempt by society to reach a proper balance between the need of the individual for protection and the necessity for a free dissemination of news and fair comment in respect to public affairs.

RIGHT OF PRIVACY

Libel is an age-old risk. The year 1890 may be said to mark the birth of its kinsman, right of privacy. As will be shown in Chapter 13, whenever a publisher or broadcaster departs from the dictates of good taste and invades this newly come right of privacy, the right is given a chance to grow, step by step, by adverse court decision. If the trend continues, a day may come when violation of right of privacy is deemed a greater danger to publishers and broadcasters than is libel.

II. HAZARDS OF LIBEL

Libel is an occupational hazard for all who communicate news, opinion, or pictures. Except as granted by statute, no publisher or broadcaster has prerogatives greater than those of the ordinary citizen.

NEWSPAPERS

Risk of libel cannot wholly be avoided by a newspaper that reports the news and dares to fight for honest government.

Deadlines demand fast handling and do not permit an exhaustive and scientific investigation of every fact. Sometimes a paper's duty to its community requires exposure of corruption under overt threat of suit by someone who thinks it will be impossible to prove in open court the facts which a reporter has unearthed, or even those which have become notorious.

Reports of crimes, trials, politics, public affairs, and many other stories involving defamation must be published. Neither reporters nor proofreaders are infallible; errors creep in. There is a day-to-day hazard that no newspaper worth reading can completely escape. It is big in terms of dollars.

RADIO AND TELEVISION

The risks of libel when broadcasting spot news are about the same. Broadcasters face additional hazards inherent in the possibility of departure from script and in Federal Communications Commission regulations pertaining to political broadcasts. These are considered in Chapters 14 and 15.

Though broadcasters do not editorialize and advocate for or against public measures as much as do newspapers, magazines, and books, the rules of fair comment and criticism reviewed in Chapter 8 are of consequence. For instance, some of the patter of a disc jockey can be justified only under the theory of fair comment and criticism. His remarks are not factual; they are but his opinion, and possibly his spontaneous opinion of the moment. When gossiping about private lives, some disc jockeys give the impression of stating supposed facts not meticulously documented as to accuracy. This tendency increases the hazards of their comments.

BOOKS AND MAGAZINES

With more time to be careful, the writers and publishers of books and magazines have an advantage over those under pressure to hurry. They have a corollary burden—their libels may appear to be deliberate, hence less excusable.

The Penalty

Regardless of whether the laws of the state permit punitive damages (damages to punish the wrongdoer in addition to compensating the injured), juries do punish by large verdicts. Stable, long-established properties have been crippled as a result of one libelous comment.

Sometimes a jury is prejudiced against the publisher or his policies, or against the broadcaster. Perhaps more frequently, the jury believes that the publisher or broadcaster was wantonly careless, malicious, or so eager for circulation or listeners that he deliberately exploited false rumors of scandal.

So, where libel may enter, every publisher and broadcaster is engaged in an extra-hazardous occupation.

III. The Theme

This manual is written for all writers, copyreaders, and telegraph, sports, women's, city, and other editors, authors, announcers, commentators, admen, proofreaders, printers, and make-up men who at one stage or another handle the copy which may contain libelous matter. *They are the fourth estate.* Men processing copy may be as much to blame when a libelous statement slips by unnoticed as is the excited cub reporter who telephones a story to the newsroom, or the advertising salesman who brings in a defamatory political ad.

Most Libel Is Avoidable

Despite the dangers, all the news can be published or broadcast and a strong editorial policy maintained with little risk if the basic legal principles are remembered and observed. Knowing how to recognize and then avoid libelous statements permits publication and broadcasting of stories and justifies aggressive editorials which an uninformed person would have to kill because of fear of the unknown. Courage comes from a confidence born of knowledge. Skilled mountaineers seldom fall; weekenders often do.

The purpose here is to state enough by way of rule or illustration to enable anyone to recognize the risk of libel—*always*, if he gathers the news and writes the story; *usually*, if he sees the copy but does not himself investigate the facts. The policy of all who engage in mass communication is presumed to be:

(i) to write or pass copy or ads for publication or broadcast free of hazard;
(ii) whenever dangerous copy is observed, to call attention to the risk of libel, violation of the right of privacy, or contempt, as the case may be.

Except for management (top brass, so to speak), the only question is—is this hazardous? If the answer is yes, the doubtful material should be stricken or so earmarked that it cannot escape the attention of those whose responsibility it is to accept or reject the risk of publishing or broadcasting dangerous statements.

Responsibility of Fourth Estate

Nothing is more important to the maintenance of a free society than the preservation and enlargement of the right of the people to know what is happening in public affairs—and to criticize those who rule them. The tendency of the executive branch of government is aggrandizement of power. The trend of the legislative is to impose ever increasing restrictions. A function of the judicial branch is to protect constitutional liberties.

Despite vexations and tribulations such as those inherent in the reporting of affairs criminal, the courts firmly uphold freedom of speech as assured in the Bill of Rights. In so doing, the judges are sustaining their natural allies—the men and women of the fourth estate. Without the courts, the right to speak freely would wither. Without the searching scrutiny to which all branches of government are subjected by news media, the courts would not long survive as truly independent arbiters.

Though the judges have the final say, responsibility for preserving a relatively free form of government and the independence of the individual rests as much upon the fourth estate as upon the courts. Such is the high mission of all who communicate news and comment on public affairs.

This book is a tool to facilitate a more complete performance of that assignment. Because it prescribes Stop, Look, and Listen, in certain close situations the rules have been strictly construed against publishers and broadcasters. *In court, the interpretation should be more favorable than here indicated.*

CHAPTER 2

WHAT IS LIBEL?

Fore-warned, fore-armed.

CERVANTES

THE words "defame" and "defamation" include both libel and slander. If the defamation is by writing, picture (printed or televised), or cartoon, it is a libel. If it is by word of mouth, it is a slander. If over the air waves, strictly speaking it is a slander. But because of the wide coverage—in contrast to mouth to ear—broadcasts are usually tested and redress given under the legal rules pertaining to printed publications. It should be assumed that when material goes on the air it is subject to the laws of libel, which are more severe than those relating to slander.

Definitions

Copy is defamatory if it tends to harm the reputation of any person by (i) exposing him to public aversion, (ii) lowering him in the estimation of his fellows, or (iii) deterring third persons from dealing with him. A corporation, partnership, club, or other association of individuals may be defamed as such. The circumstances under which an individual is himself defamed by reference to the group as a whole will be described in Chapter 4.

Libel may stem from a story which exposes a person to hatred, contempt, ridicule, or obloquy. Words are libelous if they reflect unfavorably upon personal morality or integrity, or carry imputations which tend to damage financial standing. A story may be defamatory because it harms a person socially, although no reflection is cast upon his personal or business character. Even a criminal may be libeled, as by accusing an embezzler of kidnaping. A story reporting drunken driving may be libelous of a driver convicted only of speeding.

Still another definition—this time statutory—may help make the meaning of libel as natural as the alphabet. California puts it:

> Libel is a *false and unprivileged* publication by writing, printing, picture, effigy, or other fixed representation to the eye, which exposes any person to hatred, contempt, ridicule, or obloquy, or which causes him to be shunned or avoided, or which has a tendency to injure him in his occupation.

The negation of "false and unprivileged" by proving truth or privilege, or both, is the most frequent defense.

Types of Civil Libel

1. A libel may consist of a *statement of fact,* that is to say, a report of a particular act, omission, or condition. A story which indicates that by act or omission a person has betrayed a trust, is guilty of dishonesty, fraud, or falsehood, has been cowardly, or cruel, has been profane, has been guilty of political corruption, has refused to pay his debts, or has been guilty of a crime, can be libelous. It may be libelous to report a condition of drunkenness, insanity, loathsome disease, or illegitimacy; or to say, for instance, that a person is an infidel. Words that are in

themselves innocent, but which, as used, injure another's business, property, profession, trade, or employment, may be actionable.

2. A libel can consist of a *statement of opinion* based on facts, actual or supposed.

> To say that a person is a hypocrite, faker, crook, sneak, criminal, a "Benedict Arnold," or otherwise to characterize him adversely may be libelous, whether or not the facts on which the remark is based are known to the reader.

The propriety of the opinion, in view of the provable facts, is a matter of judgment. In the heat of a campaign or crusade certain adjectives and epithets may seem proper enough. Later, calmly viewing all of the facts, a judge or jury may hold the words defamatory.

3. An *indirect statement or imputation* can be libelous if susceptible of a defamatory interpretation. Words written in jest may be read as libelous. Satire, irony, figure of speech, and innuendo may be defamatory, though not so intended.

An insinuation might be as actionable as a positive assertion, if the meaning is plain. Allusion, irony, and questions are within the bar if the defamatory inference is inherent. As a New York court put it:

> A man cannot libel another, by the publication of language, the meaning and damaging effect of which is clear to all men, and where the identity of the person meant cannot be doubted, and then escape liability through the use of a question mark.

DISPARAGEMENT OF PROPERTY—SLANDER OF TITLE—TRADE LIBEL

A story disparaging another's property (whether land, buildings, chattels, or intangible things, such as a copyright), under such circumstances that it should have been foreseen that a purchaser or lessee of the property might be influenced adversely, may give rise to a cause of action in favor of the owner for the resulting pecuniary loss.

ILLUSTRATIONS

1. Published or broadcast in good faith, a story says that many titles in Grey Acre Subdivision are defective. That is not true. The title to the property has been disparaged, slandered. The owner proves that sales were lost. Unless the story is privileged, he is entitled to damages.

2. The women's page or morning broadcast says that a particular method of canning renders food unwholesome. Jones is a canner. His advertising and labels show that he uses that method. There has been a trade libel. His business falls off. The broadcaster or publisher may be forced to prove the truth of his assertion.

Statements of this sort usually differ from a true libel which reflects on the character of the owner or operator, as when a boarding house is called a brothel. The National Broadcasting Company learned the hard way that if a trade libel goes beyond disparagement and imparts fraud or deceit it becomes actionable without proof of special damage. During a telecast one of the performers displayed to his audience an object purporting to be a package of plaintiff's product, "Ezoons." He said: "Ezoons is full of all kinds of habit-forming drugs. Nothing short of hospital care will make you stop taking Ezoons. You'll feel like a run-down hound dog and lose weight." This was a libel per se of the corporate manufacturer.

A charitable corporation or a cooperative can be libeled. Because it is dependent upon public support, matters which tend to prejudice it in public esteem and to interfere with its activities may be actionable.

A leading business publication* indicates that with increasing pressures to find buyers, some vendors are yielding to the temptation to slander a competitor's product. Under a head-

* *Wall Street Journal,* Jan. 29, 1965.

line "Rumors are Flying," it is reported that more companies are waging war on hearsay. These vendettas do not often involve media, although they may do so if the rumors are reflected in ads or news releases. Mention is made here merely to alert publishers to the possibility of an unlikely impact.

CRIMINAL LIBEL

Defamations tend to disturb the peace. They make men fighting mad. Thus, the state, as custodian of the peace, is interested. A libel may be a crime in addition to giving rise to a civil action in favor of the person defamed. Loosely defined, a criminal libel is a malicious or wanton publication of defamatory statements or pictures. In contrast to civil libel, truth cannot be relied upon as a defense against an accusation of criminal libel.

Defamation of the dead may be a criminal libel but does not ordinarily give rise to a civil action. No further reference will be made to criminal libel; if the publisher avoids flagrant civil libel, he will be safe from criminal charges. Nor will seditious libel, which tends toward treason, be touched upon.

MEANING OF WORDS

In testing for libel, the meaning of language is not limited to orthodox dictionary definition. It hinges also upon the temper of the times, colloquialisms, connotations, previous and subsequent articles or broadcasts, and matters of common knowledge in the circulation or listening area.

Meaning reflects the whole picture in relation to day and place of publication or broadcast and probable day and place of trial should a suit be brought. Context enters into meaning.

Therefore it must be remembered that the words used will be read or heard in the framework of the public knowledge.

ILLUSTRATION

To say that Joe Doakes, the gifted photographer, was having a hilarious time after five highballs would not, under most circumstances, be libelous of Joe. But to say that Joseph H. Doakes was enjoying similar festivities might be a libel per se if the reader or listener might reasonably conclude the reference to be to the Reverend Joseph H. Doakes, the eminent pastor of the First Baptist Church.

I Did Not Mean To

"I did not mean it that way" may not help. If some readers can naturally and reasonably understand a story to be defamatory, then it may be.

Standing alone, the statement, "Smith got rich fast" would not imply corruption. But the assertion, "Smith got rich fast while he was a tax collector," or the words "got rich fast" used in a context where it is implicit that Smith is or was the tax collector might well be libelous per se.

Interpretation is always in relation to time, place, and circumstances. Presently it is libelous per se to call a man a Communist. But that was not necessarily so while Russia was our ally. The time may again come when it is not so.

Judges will not strip words to their minimum meaning and ignore unfavorable implications. They will not strain to interpret pictures and cartoons in their mildest and most inoffensive sense in order to hold them not libelous.

"Publisher," "Media," "Broadcast"

Unless the defamation is "published" (communicated) to at least one third person, there is no "publication" and hence no libel. The words are in quotation to emphasize that when used alone in this book, "publisher," "publishing," and "publication" are words of art. Each includes whoever communicates orally or visually over the air or by script, printing, drawings, photographs, or any other device—a statue for example—which conveys a message. "Media" means the customary communicators—newspapers, radio, magazines, and television. The dictionary, trade custom, and the courts justify the use of the words "broadcast" and "broadcasters" to include both oral and visual broadcasts, and they are here so used.

Unless the context requires otherwise, words such as "copy," "reporter," "writer," "story," and so on apply to both publication and broadcast. For most rules considered herein, it does not matter whether the copy appears in type or is put on the air.

INNOCENT DISSEMINATION

Publication means communication—dissemination—of the libel. Innocent dissemination is a defense open only to persons who, innocently, have played a subsidiary part in the publication of the libel. It is of value to the distributor of magazines and newspapers, the bookseller, and anyone else who can establish that:

(i) he disseminated the work without knowing that it contained a libel; and

(ii) there was nothing in the work or in the circumstances which ought to have led him to suppose that it contained a libel; and

(iii) his lack of knowledge of the libel was not due to negligence on his part.

This defense may not be relied upon by printers—not even to job shops printing small items. It does not shield anyone in a position to exercise judgment or discretion in respect to content.

THE POST OFFICE

The possibility of being excluded from the mails should not be entirely forgotten. The postman is one channel of communication. His regulations are to the effect that "any libelous, scurrilous, defamatory, or threatening language" will be excluded from the mails if it appears on the outside wrapper or envelope. Headlines may be readable, for instance, through a transparent wrapper.

CHAPTER 3

KEEP AWAY FROM
LIBEL PER SE

A man defames his neighbor at his peril.

POLLOCK

THE term "per se" means "by or in itself." When the defamation is evident from the article itself, it is called a libel per se.

A libel per se is actionable per se; in itself it is a sufficient basis for a cause of action. Plaintiff need not allege or prove that he suffered actual dollar damage. In some states punitive damages (damages to punish defendant) are also allowed. The consequence is that the publisher or broadcaster must prove truth, or show privilege or other sufficient defense. The plaintiff is not required to prove the falsity. These are the dangerous libels.

In sharp contrast to libel per se, in unusual circumstances the most innocent-sounding copy may be defamatory. Suppose a story in print or over the air tells of the fine pitching of Jim Good at Saturday's sand-lot game. It should have said "Friday." If Jim is a leader in a church that makes Saturday the Sabbath, and forbids sports on a holy day, Jim may be libeled. But this is not a libel per se. Jim must demonstrate the defamation and prove that he suffered special harm.

These mild libels are difficult to recognize when editing script and reading copy or proof. They are not often important. Almost always a correction will cure the ill.

Except when management is evaluating risk, it should be assumed that anything which appears to be libelous may be libelous per se. If the publisher believes that a story is of public importance, he may decide that although apparently defamatory, the statement is not a libel per se and may be broadcast or published because (even though libelous) it seems unlikely that the plaintiff could prove he had suffered damage.

For other purposes the definitions of defamatory copy and pictures and all of the descriptions of types of civil libel found in Chapter 2 should be used as the measure of libel per se.

EXPRESSIONS LIBELOUS PER SE

Here classified are a few specific expressions typical of those which should be considered libelous per se when referring to:

Affiliations
    atheist
    Communist
    Fascist
    Ku Klux Klan
    Nazi
    nudist
    subversive groups
    any organization which, at the moment, is opprobrious
Attorneys
    ambulance chaser
    betrayed client
    hypocrite and altered records
    lacks requisite qualifications to practice
    pettifogging shyster
    shady

Attorneys—Cont.
    shyster or shysterism
    tricky and dishonest
    unprofessional conduct
Authors and journalists
    attacks sanctity of home and desecrates memory of the
        dead
    defender of degenerates for hire
    humbug and fraud
    plagiarist
    rewrote another's work
Business establishments—corporations
    ad a fraud
    adulteration of products
    complicity in swindle
    dirty products
    driven out competitors and mercilessly robbed the people
    false weights used
    filthy and unhealthful milk
    financially weak
    hot, dirty, and poorly ventilated
    precarious existence, not able to meet its financial obliga-
        tions
    price wrecker
    racketeering methods
    refuses to pay debts
    swindle
    unpaid claims
    wares worthless
Businessmen
    bankrupt
    blackmail
    crook
    defrauding government
    evading payment of a debt
    false representations
    false weights used
    fraud
    gouged money

Businessmen—Cont.
  sharp dealing
  short in accounts
Candidates, officeholders, politicians
  buys votes
  campaign of abuse and slander
  "Communist-line paper" supports him
  corruption
  deadbeat running for office for money
  debauched the electorate with liquor
  defaulter and bad moral character
  dishonest treasury raid
  falsifier of public documents
  fawning sycophant
  filching money from public
  grafter
  grossest dereliction of duty, if not crime
  groveling office seeker
  judge was a peril to children and sympathetic with crimi-
    nals
  partner of notorious criminal
  paid dollars for office
  perjurer
  pockets public funds
  received dollars for offices
  reprehensible means used in campaign
  scoundrel
  sells his influence
  sold out to the monopoly
  solicited slush funds
  stuffed the ballot box
  swindler
  superintendent of an institution permitted vile and im-
    moral conditions
Clergymen
  conduct unbecoming a married man and minister
  curses, drinks, gambles
  disgraceful conduct
  intimate with choir leader

Clergymen—Cont.

    trouble with women

    unmannerly, discourteous, and ignorant

Crimes

    any words imputing a crime regarded by the public as involving moral turpitude (petty misdemeanors, such as overtime parking or jaywalking, are excepted)

    connivance with crime

    consort with criminals

    extortion

Disease

    any loathsome disease

    any acute mental disorder

    venereal diseases

Doctors or dentists

    abortionist

    advertising specialist

    caused death by reckless treatment

    charlatan

    drug addict

    faker

    fee exorbitant and operation unnecessary

    malpractice

    neglected patient

    quack

    unprofessional conduct

    used improper instruments

Domestic difficulties

    another wife elsewhere

    divorce action instituted (i.e., when none had been)

    having wife trouble

    reference to a controversy concerning custody of children as though divorce suit is pending, when actually completed and a parent mentioned in story has remarried

Drunkenness or liquor

    aiding moonshiners

    booze hound

    drunkard

Drunkenness or liquor—Cont.
  kept booze for unlawful purposes
  toper
Honesty (see also *Reputation*)
  con man
  crook
  dishonesty
  fraud
  guilty of falsehood
  liar
  rogue
  unreliable and does not meet his obligations
  unworthy of credit
Hotels, apartments, and boarding houses
  brothel
  disorderly house
  gambling house
  vice den
Labor and management
  company put on unfair list
  company violated its union contract
  employer falsified facts to workers and the public
  racketeers
  scab
  strikebreaker and foe of labor
  union officials corrupt
Morality
  adulterer
  affinity
  bigamist
  fornication
  homosexual or a queer
  illicit relations
  infidelity
  lovemate
  mistress
  moral delinquency
  moral obliquity

Morality—Cont.
promiscuous lovemaker
seducer
unmarried mother
unchastity
villain

Obituaries (person not dead)
death in discreditable circumstances
suicide, or other disgraceful cause

Patriotism
anarchist
flag, called it a dirty rag
red-tinted agitator
secret foreign agent
seditious agitator
spreader of distrust, discontent, and sedition
traitor

Reputation (see also *Honesty*)
deadbeat
disreputable
gambler
horse thief
hypocrite
illegitimate
jumped his board bill
low grade creature of crass ignorance and stupid egotism
no honorable reason for . . .
poltroon
rascal
skunk
suicide attempted
venality
vile and slanderous tongue
wastrel

Sanity
fit to be sent to asylum
just a little daft
unsafe to be at large
unsound mind

Teachers
   double-talk by school official
   ignoramus
   incompetent
   intemperate
   shameless skulduggery
   unfit to be on faculty
   unladylike conduct, unfit to teach school
This and that
   blasphemy, guilty of
   community cannot despise him more
   deprived of ordinances of the church
   ejected by police (the reference being to a reputable
      citizen)
   informer
   infringed a patent
   insulted females
   juror agreed to determine verdict by lot
   juror agreed to determine verdict by game of checkers
   jurors did injustice to oaths
   libelous journalist
   publisher of a libel
   suicide, in reference to a living person
   uses cloak of religion for unworthy purposes

All of the foregoing words and expressions should be considered libelous per se. However, *as a matter of defense,* under
special circumstances not to be relied upon in advance, certain
of them may be held not libelous per se. For instance, a state
supreme court held it not libelous per se to call a candidate a liar
when referring only to his campaign ads and not to him as a person. The judges slapped the wrists of the writer and the editor
by remarking that the word is "unbecoming of a reputable
newspaper."

RECAPITULATION

Specific false expressions such as those just listed (all included in the types of libel described in Chapter 2) may be reclassified into four kinds of libel per se:

1. Accusations or imputations of crime.
2. Statements or insinuations of insanity or of loathsome or contagious disease.
3. Assertions of want of capacity to conduct one's business or profession.
4. Any expression which tends to bring public hatred, contempt, or ridicule.

Sinister Conduct Inferred

The fact that a matter is viewed as newsworthy supports the inference that something of special importance is being communicated. The classic example is that of the mate who truthfully wrote in the ship's log: "Captain sober today." It is a libel per se to accuse a captain of drunkenness when aboard ship.

Arsenic and Old Lace

A Boston newspaper ran an article stating that the hospital suspected that Mary Perry's husband (whose death was being probed) suffered from chronic arsenic poisoning. The writer embellished this provable fact, in itself not particularly significant, by adding: (i) decedent's brother had died approximately a month later after having spent two days "here" for the funeral, (ii) Mary's mother had died after she came to live with her daughter and her remains were cremated, and (iii) decedent was Mary's second husband.

Remarks (i), (ii), and (iii) are innocent whether read severally or collectively. But why include them in a story saying that the autopsy "disclosed that 500 times the usual amount of arsenic was in his hair?"

The court of appeals answered in language most elegant:

Taking the article as a whole we believe it would be only natural for readers to assume that they were being furnished with something more than necrology, or trivia concerning the relict of a routinely posted cadaver, and that they could well conclude that the plaintiff was suspected of having engaged in highly sinister conduct.

The lesson is that the very act of sensationalizing an otherwise innocent story may make it a libel per se.

CHAPTER 4

INTENTION
AND MISTAKE

Hell is paved with good intentions.

SAMUEL JOHNSON

MOST libel actions stem from careless reporting or writing or from loose treatment in the course of editing, printing, or broadcasting—including departures from script. Many a libel comes from what may be termed unimaginative handling of a routine story, i.e., no one noticed that, while superficially innocent of libel, the story was actually libelous per se. Attempts to build a story out of little or nothing involve disproportionate risks.

GOOD INTENTIONS

If the words are susceptible to a defamatory meaning, the copy or script might be libelous despite the most innocent of motives. The publisher or broadcaster may be liable even though:

(i) the writer carefully gathered data and believed them to be true;

   (ii) he did not intend the story to be read in a defamatory sense;

  (iii) he did not realize that it could be so understood;

  (iv) the libel was caused by typographical error or a slip of the tongue;

   (v) the words or pictures were fictional—not referring to anyone;

  (vi) all was in jest—no harm intended;

 (vii) no copyreader, continuity editor, proofreader, or anyone else suspected defamation.

If even a minority of readers, listeners, or viewers could reasonably interpret the story or picture as defamatory, the court or jury may so construe it. When words are ambiguous, the jury may be allowed to consider testimony of hearers or readers as to how they understood them. That gives plaintiff's friends a golden opportunity.

Good faith is of course a defensive aid. In contrast, if anyone preparing, passing upon, or handling copy has been negligent in failing to observe discernible error, the defendants in the libel case have two strikes against them.

HEADLINES

Defamatory headlines may not be cured by explanations in the story. The courts realize that frequently the reader catches the headlines, then reads the article itself so hastily that he fails to grasp fine distinctions.

CAUTION
Because of their brevity, headlines may be ambiguous. When the story itself is close to being dangerous, the headlines must be watched with special care.

Misuse of headlines occurs most frequently in connection with reports of criminal investigations. "Murderer Apprehended," "Kidnaper Caught," "Sheriff Nabs Thief," and the like may be libelous though followed (it might be said because followed) by a story that states explicitly that the suspect has only been arrested or charged and stoutly maintains his innocence.

ILLUSTRATIONS

1. One newspaper suffered a large verdict for its headline, "Spy Caught." A competitive paper escaped liability because its headline was, "Arrested Aboard Ship as Spy."

2. A headline saying, "Doctor Kills Child," was followed by a story of an auto accident in which the doctor driver was perhaps negligent but certainly not deliberately reckless. The headline misled. It connoted intent or unprofessional conduct.

3. The headline was "Babies for Sale . . . Trade of Child Told." The tagline read, "Tomorrow—Blackmail by Franklin." The body of the article accurately recited the facts concerning the adoption in question. The publisher contended that the headline and tagline cannot be considered apart from the context in which they were used. The Supreme Court of Nevada answered: "This is not so . . . the public frequently reads only the headlines."

A wire service is not liable for headlines added by a newspaper.

IDENTIFICATION

Although the writer and all others passing upon copy or script honestly believe the reference is applicable only to a certain person, there is not sufficient excuse if, in fact, the public may reasonably think the story applies to another person. The test is not whom the story intends to name but who a part of the audience may reasonably think is named—"not who is meant but who is hit," as one court put it.

ILLUSTRATIONS

Acquaintances might be able to identify an unnamed subject from:

1. "Veteran's wife says he beat her and year-old triplets."
2. "Mr. Rothschild, the bank's president, believes that a newly employed watchman is implicated in the robbery."

A story in the *Chicago Tribune* told of a vice raid. Dolores Reising, fifty-seven, alias Eve Spiro and Eve John, was named as the suspected keeper of the apartment. Plaintiff was twenty-seven years of age. She resided in an apartment below the one raided. Her maiden name had been Eve Spiro and her name at the time, although she was divorced, was Eve John. She was in no way involved in the raid or the immoral activities of her landlady. The Supreme Court of Illinois held that the story was not "of and concerning" the twenty-seven-year-old; she was not libeled.

Libelous things were published about the conduct of a corporation, but no officer was mentioned. The president sued. He proved that it was well known that he controlled the corporation; ergo, the townsfolk understood that he had been charged with the nefarious acts. He was allowed recovery without proof of special damage. *Query:* Would not the result have been the same if the public had thought him to be the boss even though he was a mere figurehead in the corporate affairs?

A telecast sponsored by the Better Business Bureau defamed the "Day and Night Television Service." Suit was brought by the two partners, although neither had been named and one was a silent partner, not active in the business. The libel of the trade name was held a libel of the two partners, either of whom was entitled to maintain the successful action against the broadcasting company.

When a person is identified by address, vocation, hobby (such as archery), relatives, or other data, the indicia, if in error, may make the story libelous. Suppose a story says that Bill Brown, former football star, was arrested for drunken driving. The name is correct, but the deputy sheriff was in error as to the football. The story libels the football star of that name.

CAUTION
If a coined name is used, make sure it will not fit some living person or that it is obviously a "John Doe" type of name, not applicable to anyone in particular.

But the persons named must be sufficiently identified. Otherwise someone else of that name may be able to state a cause of action. A defamatory statement names Richard Roe of Milwaukee, without further identification. Three Richard Roes live in that city. Two of them might be in a position to state a cause of action for a libel even though the story is true as to the third.

It should not be assumed that similarity in names means identity.

LIBEL BY REFERENCE TO A CLASS

An individual may be defamed by words which disparage a small group of which he is a member, as by a statement that "the members of the school board are corrupt." Hence, fine discrimination must be exercised when deciding whether a reference to a small body of people (or to an unnamed member or members thereof) identifies particular persons.

The size of the group is a critical, but not necessarily the controlling, factor. Obviously a reference to "a corrupt Congressman" or to "corrupt Congressmen" does not in itself identify anyone in that huge body. But a libelous statement referring to the congressional delegation from a named state, particularly a small state, might be actionable by some or all of those congressmen.

ILLUSTRATION
Assume a board of twelve city councilmen and, in the same area, a board of three county commissioners. Accusa-

tions of graft in city and county government may require different treatments.

GROUP LIBEL

Statutory libel of the group itself is in sharp contrast to libel of an individual by reference to his group. An occasional law prohibits any publication or broadcast which, for instance, "would expose citizens of any race, creed, or color to contempt, derision, or obloquy." Such restrictions are primarily penal.

SUCCESSIVE STORIES

In a succession of stories, a person may be libeled by a story in which he is not named and from which story (if read alone) he cannot be identified, if he is named or identified in a previous or subsequent story. Hence, all of a series must be read together for the purpose of determining possible libel and identification.

ILLUSTRATION

Anxious to acquire funds to finance law school, two students evolved an elaborate abduction-robbery scheme to plunder a liquor store. Plans went awry. Harry was caught hiding under burlap sacks in the store. He confessed, giving details other than the identity of his accomplice. The case was novel, and open and shut as to Harry. Media ran stories sufficient to convince readers of the guilt of both.

Later David was charged. If (i) the second series of stories names David in contrast to "student held," and (ii) David pleads not guilty and is acquitted, the series of stories defames a legally innocent aspirant to the bar.

MALICE FROM CARELESSNESS

In the eyes of the jury carelessness merges into recklessness. They both feed a charge of malice. For practical purposes it is not necessary to delve into what constitutes malice—actual and constructive. Technical legal rules as to whether and when plaintiff must allege and prove malice are bypassed here. Suffice it to say that if the tone of a story or comment or the circumstances of publication or broadcast indicate malice toward the plaintiff, the jury will be slow to believe the defenses and might be lavish in the verdict.

A pungent definition is that as an ingredient of an action for libel, "malice signifies nothing more than a wrongful act done intentionally, without just cause or excuse."

Negligent Mistake

Occasionally a publisher is threatened with litigation bottomed on the negligent publication of an untrue statement which is *not* libelous. Most of the reported cases which originate in the news columns stem from false reports of death, bringing anxiety to those who believe themselves bereaved. Some decisions recognize a "duty if one speaks at all," to give correct information.

Errors in ads are more apt to be false figures than a misstatement of text—a bargain at "$9.95" when the copy read "$19.95." Sometimes a correction pacifies the advertiser and his customers; sometimes not. A directive from general management to the store managers of one of the largest national outlets is essentially: "Store go ahead and sell at advertised price; if media are responsible for incorrect price, description, etc., we will pass loss on sales back to newspaper or station." Of course, each instance must be handled in its own framework.

An item to remember: If the error is bad enough, the store's customers could not be misled. Assume, for instance, the picture of a mink stole normally selling for, say, $850. The copy carried a bargain price of $695. If the printed ad or broadcast puts the price at $395, the advertising department is in trouble. The ladies will flock in to buy the stole at $395. But if the mistake is so gross that no sensible person should be misled, the publisher is in an embarrassing but not so serious situation.

A published price of $99.95 for that stole should alert everyone to the fact that a mistake has been made. In contrast, if the mistake were a reduction to $395, the store might well feel obligated to honor its ad, with consequent damages assessable to the publisher in addition to the running of a corrected ad.

A suit based on negligent mistake with no allegation of libel seldom finds its way to a supreme court. Actual damage resulting from news stories is rare and hard to prove. Certainly, however, a justified complaint concerning a negligent news story gives the cue for a prompt and clear correction, if feasible, in a manner desired by the persons who claim injury.

CHAPTER 5

QUOTATIONS AND ADS

Tale-bearers are as bad as the tale-makers.

SHERIDAN

PUBLISHERS and broadcasters may not repeat false and defamatory matter and escape liability with the plea that they were but quoting a source deemed authentic or passing along current news already published or on the air. They are not saved by naming the author or origin, or even by accompanying the defamation with an expression of disbelief.

QUOTATIONS

Except in a very few situations (there is occasional statutory relief) they may be held liable for publication or broadcast of items received through the news services. They may be responsible for what their columnists and commentators say, despite disavowal of sponsorship and disagreement with the statements made and views expressed.

Truth, privilege, fair comment, and other defenses are of course available. But *in the absence of privilege,* the defense of truth requires more than merely proving that the quoted statement was made by someone else. The jury must be satisfied that the defamatory assertions are substantially correct.

ILLUSTRATION
At a community club meeting an indignant citizen asserted that a certain officeholder "pockets public funds." This was repeated by the press and over the air. Libel suits ensued. A host of witnesses testified that those very words had been used. Such testimony does not prove truth. The occasion being unprivileged, the defendants must convince each juror that plaintiff did pocket public funds.

If the source of the story is such that some privilege may attach, that source should be identified, as by name and office. The loose expression "high officials state" is a weak foundation upon which to build a defense of privilege. Reference to a proper specific source shows authenticity and the propriety of relying upon that source.

ILLUSTRATION
For cause of death, quote "J. B.' Ded, King County Coroner," if possible, rather than someone in another department. If the story has to do with an investigation of graft or faulty construction in the erection of the new city hall, quote the Mayor or head of the Board of Public Works, not a councilman, unless he has special responsibilities or is known to be well informed.

The stock phrases "it is alleged," "it is reported," "police say," and so on are meaningless so far as liability for defamation is concerned unless the story is actually privileged.

It distills almost to this: In the absence of qualified privilege, one who repeats another's defamatory remarks is legally responsible unless he has available defenses which would shield him were he the author.

ADVERTISEMENTS

When passing upon advertising copy and script, apply the general rules pertaining to libel. In addition, the possibility of disparaging (libeling) the property or business of a third party must be kept in mind (see Chapter 2, Trade Libels). Unnamed individuals may be identified by reference to their business or trade name. The ad that appears on the screen in a telecast should be scrutinized, as well as the script that the announcer will read.

An advertiser is permitted to push his own merchandise or services until he approaches the border lines of fraud and misrepresentation. However, his promotions must be by way of praise of his own product, not by disparagement of his competitor.

STATUTES

In some states there are statutes imposing artificial, in contrast to common law, restrictions upon advertising. Indeed, legislation of this sort is sometimes found in city ordinances with municipal, but not statewide, effect. Local counsel should be consulted in these matters.

Likewise, advertising must conform to postal regulations—in respect, for instance, to lotteries.

ADS CONCERNING PUBLIC OFFICIALS

Paid political ads are within the privilege protecting those who—without malice—make factual errors when criticizing the conduct of public officials. Were this not so, "editorial advertisements" would be discouraged and thus shut off an important outlet for the promulgation of information and ideas by persons who do not themselves have access to the press and the air waves.

Following a like rule previously adopted by a number of states, in the *New York Times* case (1964) the Supreme Court of the United States held that constitutional guarantees prohibit "a public official from recovering damages for a defamatory falsehood *relating to his official conduct* unless he proves that the statement was made with actual malice—that is, with knowledge that it was false or with reckless disregard of whether it was false or not" (emphasis added).

This sound rule may trap the unwary. It is not a license to print or broadcast any political ad concerning an officeholder. Perhaps responsible personnel do know of the falsity, and the circumstances are such that their knowledge will be imputed to the publisher. Or careless handling of copy may influence a judge or jury to find that there was a reckless disregard of whether or not the ad was false.

Note well the phrase "relating to his official conduct." A frequent vice of political advertising—particularly during campaigns—is to purport to expose the private life of the officeholder or otherwise attack him in respect to matters not related to his official conduct.

Ads Concerning Candidates

The privilege described in the preceding section applies to ads attacking officeholders. It would seem that public policy requires a like latitude regarding the qualifications of a candidate for public office. Some decisions indicate that such is or will become the law.

At present, however, it is prudent to assume that the publisher may be put to the burden of proving the truth of libelous assertions concerning a candidate not yet in office.

The compressed coverage of the qualified privilege pertaining to political ads is included in this chapter only as an aid to quick reference. A study of Chapters 6, 7, and 8 is essential to an understanding of what has been said here.

Practical Politics

Not infrequently a campaign committee offers a libelous or a borderline ad with the assertion that "this has been approved by our attorney and he says it is safe." If the copy is plainly libelous per se, it should not be run or broadcast unless management is on a crusade, is confident the assertions are true or privileged, and knowingly assumes the risk.

If, however, there is some question as to whether it is safe, and the people are responsible and solvent, a practical out is to suggest to the committee:

> You, of course, have confidence in your attorney. Our attorney is doubtful, but you have a greater factual background, and he may be unduly apprehensive. If all members of the committee and their wives will enter into an agreement to pay our expenses incident to trial and to indemnify us if any judgment should be entered against us, we will be glad to print or broadcast your ad.

Almost always this ends the matter and snuffs out criticism to the effect that the publisher or broadcaster is too timid.

Political ads may be subject to statutory requirements touching identification of sponsors and related matters.

Ads on the Air

The provisions of the Communications Act are such that the station has "no power of censorship over the material broadcast by a qualified candidate." Ordinary rules do not apply. The content of advertising time bought by or on behalf of candidates for public office comes within the principles and regulations described in Chapters 14 and 15.

BIENNIAL REFRESHERS

Most political ads come in election years—perhaps biennially. Admen are not constantly faced with libel, as are reporters and the writers of editorials. The advertising staff may not be libel conscious, and ads can slip by which would be refused if read with discernment. A salesman who has been on the job for a year and a half—between elections—considers himself experienced, yet he may never have handled libelous copy. In fairness to advertising personnel, it is suggested that they are entitled to a refresher on libel before each hot campaign.

REFUSAL TO ACCEPT ADVERTISING

The public has a strong interest in the operation of newspapers and magazines. However, the courts usually hold that publication is a private enterprise and that those who engage in it are free to deal with whomever they choose. Hence, any advertising may be refused unless the refusal furthers an illegal monopoly or other unlawful purpose.

Radio and television have broader responsibilities in respect to treating all alike when the interest of the public may be involved. Their discretion in refusing purely *commercial* advertising is as wide as that accorded other privately owned media. But because each uses an exclusive channel allocated and licensed under federal law, they have less discretion when the proffered ad is in connection with a political campaign or touches matters of public interest. Chapter 15 (Political Broadcasts) and Part II of Chapter 14 (Controversial Issues and Fair Play) cover these areas.

BILLING FOR ADS

Roughly worded follow-ups to advertisers who neglect to pay their bills may bring the business office afoul of the Post Office

Department. It forbids any mailing which has on its outside "any language asking for payment of a bill, which by its manner or style of display is defamatory and reflects injuriously on the character of addressee." Sometimes an economy-minded credit department (or its delegate, a collection agency) uses post cards, particularly for classified ads. Occasionally, over-zealous collection efforts end in libel suits against the creditor.

CHAPTER 6

PRIVILEGE—WHO HAS IT?

> *The only security of all is in a free press.*
> *. . . No government ought to be without*
> *censors: and where the press is free no one*
> *ever will.*
>
> THOMAS JEFFERSON

THE broad term "privilege" includes both absolute privilege and qualified privilege. Publishers and broadcasters enjoy no absolute privilege. For them and for all who do not qualify as actors on a stage affording absolute privilege, the word "privilege" must mean a qualified or conditional privilege. This chapter is devoted to the general nature of absolute and qualified privilege.

I. ABSOLUTE PRIVILEGE

Absolute privilege is strictly limited, both as to the persons whose utterances are protected and the occasions on which it may be invoked. It allows any statements, however erroneous and however damaging, about any person, with complete protection from accountability for the libelous utterance. It is a freedom conferred only when the rights of individuals to protection against libel must be subjugated to the common good, i.e., the individual's interest in his reputation must be sacrificed in order to permit the free functioning of the processes of government.

By-passing certain private occasions (husband-wife, priest-penitent, and a few others), the rule is that absolute privilege applies only in three general areas: (i) judicial proceedings, (ii) legislative proceedings, and (iii) the acts of important government officials, usually executives. *When statements absolutely privileged when uttered are repeated by others, the privilege becomes qualified or conditional.*

JUDICIAL PROCEEDINGS

A judge or other judicial officer, an attorney participating in a judicial proceeding, parties to litigation, witnesses, and jurors are all absolutely privileged to make false and defamatory statements during and as part of the trial, if they bear some relationship to the matter under consideration.

LEGISLATIVE PROCEEDINGS

A member of the Congress of the United States or of the legislature of any state or territory is absolutely privileged to say false and defamatory things in the performance of his legislative function. But in a lesser assembly (a town council, for instance) a member may not enjoy an absolute privilege if he is malicious or if his remarks become irrelevant to the public matter then under consideration.

GOVERNMENT OFFICIALS

The President of the United States, the governor of any state or territory, the cabinet officers of the United States, the heads of important branches of the federal government, and the corresponding officers of any state or major municipal or other government entity, are absolutely privileged when making false and defamatory statements if (i) they are made in the course of executive proceedings in which the officer is acting, and (ii) they have some relation thereto.

ILLUSTRATIONS

1. The president of the borough of Queens submitted a report to the mayor which said that plaintiff's appraisals were based on "misinformation, ignorance, distortion and incompetence." Condemnation procedures were commanding public interest. Three months later, defendant made a copy of his report available for newsmen. It was publicized. The court held: (i) The borough president acted within the scope of his official duties. He had an absolute privilege when making the libelous statements contained in his report to the mayor. (ii) Release to the press was within the scope of his absolute privilege. The report covered a matter of public concern. Upon demand, he was obliged to release this public document.

2. A highway contractor complained because a member of the highway commission said he should be barred from bidding on future jobs and that certain actions of the contractor were "premeditated, malicious and done with intent to defraud" the government. The statement was made at a meeting of the commission, with reporters present. The Supreme Court of New Mexico held that the commissioner was such an officer of the state as to be absolutely privileged if what he said had some relation to the executive proceeding in which he was participating.

3. In the course of a fracas concerning Japanese bonds, the superintendent of banks made libelous statements concerning plaintiff, formerly his attorney. They were repeated in the news reports. The Supreme Court of California held that the public statement made by the superintendent in defense of the policies of his department was in the exercise of an executive function and protected by an absolute privilege.

4. During discussion of the operation of the police department at a regularly scheduled meeting of the city council, a councilman stated that a deputy city marshal had "propositioned" a woman to whom he was issuing a traffic ticket. Finding that the remark had a reasonable relation to the subject of the meeting, the Supreme Court of Utah held the councilman protected by an absolute privilege.

5. In contrast: The acting director of the Office of Rent Stabilization went entirely outside his line of duty when he issued a press release explaining why he suspended named subordinates from their positions.

Similarly, a United States Marshal was not absolutely privileged to defame his deputies when publicly explaining his reasons for dismissing them.

Particularly in federal court, a common expression is that an official statement of an officer or employee is absolutely privileged "if made within the outer perimeter of his line of duty."

Administrative Proceedings

Absolute privilege is extended to important administrative proceedings conducted in a manner which affords safeguards customary in a judicial proceeding.

But unless these safeguards are available, an administrative hearing in the lower echelons may not create an occasion of absolute privilege. Statements made at such hearings may be slanderous and actionable, unless made in good faith, without knowledge of the falsity, and for justifiable ends.

Illustration

Congress directed the Securities and Exchange Commission to make a "study and investigation" of the rules governing national securities exchanges to determine whether the rules adequately protect investors. The SEC set up a study group to do so. During the course of a hearing held in Washington, D.C., witnesses from a leading brokerage firm slandered one Engelmohr. He brought suit against the witnesses. The Supreme Court of Washington held that the statements made by the witness at the hearing were not absolutely privileged.

In respect to all occasions of absolute privilege, for publishers the important question is: May we safely repeat what was there said? This is the transition to a qualified privilege.

II. Qualified Privilege

Sometimes statements made between two (or among a few) individuals, as between past and prospective employers of an applicant for a job, are qualifiedly privileged. The rules pertaining to these private communications are here bypassed; publishers and broadcasters are primarily interested in reporting proceedings, occasions, and matters affecting the public generally and in relaying spot news to everybody.

A qualified—a conditional—privilege arises when it is more important for the public to be informed about the privileged proceeding or event than it is for an individual to have legal redress. This most frequently occurs in connection with reports of judicial or legislative proceedings and in stories concerning the administration of government.

Anyone reporting these and other privileged occasions to the public enjoys a limited privilege. This privilege of telling about these occasions is said to be qualified or conditional because good faith and absence of malice are elements. If qualified privilege is abused, it is forfeited.

The qualifiedly privileged report need not be a verbatim account, but it must be fair and impartial. The qualified privilege applies only to that which happened and was said during the privileged occasion. If the story includes additional facts, the publisher must be prepared to prove that the added statements are true.

Maxima Confusio in Libello

The confusion which, in some states, exists in the law of libel has been noted by many writers, both judicial and lay. It is deplored by all. Explorations into the reasons leading to the confusion would end in mere speculation, not worth while here.

Significant segments of the law of libel are unique—dissimilar from legal rules with which lawyers and judges are most familiar. Libel cases are relatively few in number. Judges are not ordinarily experienced in the practical application of the basic concepts of qualified privilege and fair comment essential to the preservation of freedom of speech and, in turn, of a free society.

And so it is that here and there will be found maverick decisions which distort the law of libel. For instance, for more than a generation an appellate court repeated the whimsical refrain: "Privilege ends where falsity begins." Yet obviously the very essence of the defense of privilege is protection despite falsity.

Recently, in a five-to-four decision, the majority of a nine-judge appellate court twice said (in essence): "The defense of qualified privilege does not extend to a publication to the entire public." If that were the law, legislative and judicial proceedings could not be reported, except at prohibitive risk, without omitting defamatory remarks, no matter who made them. It is apparent that such an error cannot be permitted in a government by and for the people—the "entire public" does have a right to know.

American courts are not alone in finding defamation to be a baffling segment of the law. After a decade of study, a white-wigged committee appointed by the Lord High Chancellor of Great Britain reported a consensus of public opinion:

> The law and practice in actions for defamation are:
>   (i) unnecessarily complicated and (ii) unduly costly;

(iii) such as to make it difficult to forecast the result of an action both as to liability and as to measure of damages;

(iv) liable to stifle discussion upon matters of public interest and concern (here only we are better off than the British);

(v) too severe on a defendant who is innocent of any intention to defame; and

(vi) too favorable to those who, in colloquial language, may be described as "gold-digging" plaintiffs.

It is comparatively easy for society to decide that a negotiable instrument must, among other things, be for a sum certain in money payable to order or bearer. It is exceedingly difficult to determine under what circumstances one citizen should be permitted to malign another. Every jurisdiction is subject to oddities in the law of libel.

There is no formula that will automatically determine how much reliance may be placed upon each of the myriad variable possible occasions of qualified privilege. Typical situations must therefore be described, and a practical evaluation made. We now come to that task. Often the lone word "privilege" will be used in lieu of the longer expression "conditional or qualified privilege."

CHAPTER 7

QUALIFIED PRIVILEGE—
PRACTICAL APPLICATION

To abuse it is to lose it.

MACRAE

THE familiar rule is that a qualified privilege protects fair reports of judicial, legislative, and executive proceedings. Most qualified privilege stems from facets of those three types of absolute privilege.

I. JUDICIAL PROCEEDINGS

We now reach the conditions necessary to the utilization of qualified privilege as a defense. First comes practical application to judicial proceedings.

TRIALS

Everyone may quote false and defamatory matter made in the course of and as part of a trial in open court. Accurate and fair reports of these hearings are guarded by a privilege which is diluted only to the extent that protection is lost if the story is published for the purpose of defaming the individual named and not to inform the public. This privilege, in contrast to a weak qualified privilege, gives protection even though it is known that the defamatory statement is false.

It is applicable to coverage of proceedings in any court—federal, state, or municipal—whether it is a court of general, or of special and limited, jurisdiction. Except in the most flagrant situations, the reporter need not be concerned with whether the court has lawful jurisdiction of the particular controversy in which it undertakes to act.

The judicial proceedings within the rule are not limited to full-dress trials. But neither do they include everything that occurs as an incident to the jousts in open court. For instance, statements stricken from the record may not be privileged.

Ex Parte Hearings

Sometimes, as on a show-cause order, only one party is before the court. The other has not yet had a chance to be heard. This does not destroy privilege if the matter has come officially before the tribunal and action has been taken.

Caution

When only one side has been heard, great care should be used lest the story be unfair to the absent party. The privilege must not be abused. If possible, the explanation of the person defamed should be in the first story. When he has had his day in court, his side of the controversy should be reported.

If the person defamed is not a party to the action, an extra check should be made to be sure of identity—is this the individual to whom the judge or witness referred?

Pleadings Before Judicial Action

A great judge said that in respect to court proceedings a qualified privilege is granted not to satisfy public curiosity about a neighbor's misfortune but to enable the public to watch the court perform its judicial functions and see that justice is evenhanded. Consistent with his theory, in most states the mere filing of a complaint, petition, answer, or similar document with the clerk of the court does not in itself make the contents privileged.

Hence, unless (as in a few jurisdictions; ask your lawyer) the laws of the states in which the publication circulates or the broadcast is heard are clear to the effect that merely filing such a paper does give rise to a qualified privilege, it should be assumed that there is none.

The privilege to repeat its contents attaches when a document has been called to the attention of the court and the court has acted. Final disposition of the matter by the court is not required. It is enough if some judicial action has been taken so that in the normal progress of the proceeding a final decision will be rendered.

> Almost always, if a modicum of skill is exercised, a first-class page-one story and headline can be run or a news broadcast safely featured when the complaint or other document is first filed, even before any judicial action is taken. The parties may be named, the nature of the action and the relief sought described, and (except in very rare instances) enough of the allegations recited to round out the story. Usually the omission or toning down of specific defamatory allegations will make the publication secure.

Pleadings in abatement proceedings are subject to the rules just given.

AFFIDAVITS AND SUNDRY COURT PAPERS

What has just been said in respect to pleadings applies generally to affidavits, exhibits, evidentiary instruments, and so on filed with the clerk but not yet presented to the judge.

Sometimes a zealous reporter (we hope discreetly) programs with counsel to the end that the newsworthy item is brought to the attention of the court for action—of course at a propitious hour in relation to deadlines. Then the story is privileged, though perhaps subject to attack for abuse of privilege.

> *A possible situation:* The reporter and lawyer who seeks publicity for his case connive for privilege for a sensational story. The suit fails and, in due course, the opposing party commences a counter-offense based on malicious prosecution. Has the publisher conspired with the reckless lawyer to publicize a malicious and unfounded proceeding and thus become a conspirator?

CORONER'S JURY

The actual verdict of a coroner's jury is privileged unless it is apparent that the procedure was irregular, that the verdict was not reached in good faith, or that it contains defamatory matter not pertinent to the inquiry. Sometimes the inquiry before a coroner's jury is one-sided with no chance for an accused to be heard. Sometimes the accused is present and is afforded an opportunity to testify and examine witnesses. Accordingly, when an inquest is reported, discrimination must be used.

> ### CAUTION
> If, for instance, a verdict reads, "Death by poisoning," but does not name the person who administered the vial, disproportionate risk is assumed if the suspected person is

named, unless the story gives a fair and impartial account of his testimony.

GRAND JURIES

A grand jury conducts a secret inquisition. There is no carte blanche to repeat everything said before or reported by a grand jury, even after its indictment or report has been presented to the court.

Some grand juries have statutory power to investigate public institutions and other public affairs and to make reports concerning them. Other grand juries—including federal—have only the right to indict or ignore; such a jury has no right to make a report of any kind. Its "report" might have no privilege at all, except as a matter of great public importance and concern. When publishing the report of a grand jury, know whether the latitude is present which follows a report directed or authorized by statute. When excerpts are published, be sure it is done fairly, without libelous implications running beyond the privileged report.

The news story may say that the grand jury was critical of, or severely condemned, the subject of its inquiry, but should not recite libelous details unless clearly in the public interest or included in an indictment.

CAUTION

Grand jury reports containing libelous imputations upon private citizens or upon public officers not touching their fitness for office or their fidelity to the public service or the propriety of official acts must be handled circumspectly.

The indictments may be described and those indicted named. The story may of course be rounded out to the extent proper whenever a criminal charge is filed against a person presumably innocent.

INDICTMENTS, INFORMATIONS, WARRANTS FOR ARREST

There is a qualified privilege when publishing the charge contained in an information, indictment, or warrant for arrest. Here privilege combines with the easily provable truth that the charge was actually filed, as long (but only as long) as the story stays by the court record. Often the off-the-record statements of law enforcement officers contain real news, but, as will be seen, except in rare instances these carry little or no privilege.

CAUTIONS

1. It should be remembered that a suspect is presumed innocent until proved guilty. It may be proper to say, "Jones was arrested and questioned" but libelous to say, "Burglar is caught" or "Hunted criminal is found." When no indictment, information, or warrant has been issued, the story should usually be limited to a statement such as, "Blank was arrested and is being held" in connection with the case.

2. Expressions such as "suspect grilled" should not be used until a charge has been filed. The suspect may be exonerated, never charged with crime, and then may sue, claiming that he was being questioned only as a possible witness.

3. If it is manifest that the charging officer has gone beyond the customary language of a charge and, for instance, unnecessarily maligned third persons, the material should be handled charily.

Reports of the preliminary proceedings before the magistrate as well as of the trial itself are privileged.

POLICE NEWS

Strictly speaking, police news emanates from an administrative arm of government. Because it usually attends or precedes a judicial proceeding, we treat it here.

The suspicions and theories, the clues and forecasts, and the reports of law enforcement officers seeking publicity often accompany criminal charges. These statements are not privileged. Privilege must be based on one or more of the several occasions already discussed.

CAUTION

The report by an officer that the prisoner has confessed is not privileged. It may be true, but sometimes a prisoner denies that he confessed. The publisher must be prepared to prove that the confession was made. Confessions that implicate others have added hazards.

Sometimes confessions are lost by the police. In dubious cases it is prudent to photograph the confession so that it will be available when needed.

Much study has been given by bench, bar, and the fourth estate to the handling of news of crimes. Chapter 16 is devoted to freedom of speech vis-à-vis fair trials.

DEPOSITIONS

Ordinarily, depositions of parties or witnesses are not privileged until read in court or the contents otherwise brought to the attention of the judge for action. Beware of depositions released by publicity-conscious lawyers prior to presentation in court.

II. LEGISLATIVE PROCEEDINGS

The virile type of qualified privilege applicable to judicial proceedings in open court extends its protection to fair reports of legislative debate and action.

ON THE FLOOR

If the distinguished senator from Utah forgets senatorial courtesy and when the Senate is in session says defamatory things about the distinguished senator from New York, the people have a right to know of the fracas. A fair account may be published locally or broadcast to every hamlet in the Empire State without fear of actionable libel. The protection is the same, regardless of whom the senator attacks from the floor of the Senate, or a representative defames from the floor of the House.

The privilege protects a story when it tells of the official proceedings of any state legislature. It applies also, but not necessarily with full force, to the official proceedings of a city or town council, school board, county commissioners, or other official municipal body. But discretion must be used when repeating irrelevant libels uttered before minor legislative groups.

CAUTION

Recall the periodic challenge of one legislator to another to "say that off the floor so I can sue you for libel"? The privilege attaches to official proceedings, not to personal vendettas outside the legislative hall.

Impeachment proceedings are within the privilege.

COMMITTEE HEARINGS

Committees are part of the legislative process. Some hearings are conducted with pomp and paraphernalia comparable to an important court proceeding. Some are informal. Some are secret.

Certainly a vigorous qualified privilege attaches to reports of a formal legislative hearing, open to the public. In contrast, discretion must be used when reciting what the reporter believes happened (impeccable but unnamed sources) at a hearing where the public was barred. The official report of the committee is privileged; a leak as to what the report will say is not. If defamatory, it is dangerous. The report itself may be different.

What has just been said applies to the committees of the Con-

57

gress, state legislatures, and important municipal legislative bodies—including port commissions, school boards, sewer or water or flood commissions, and so on. As the status descends from the Congress to the municipal level, increasing care must be taken to make sure that the hearing meets the basic tests necessary to a foundation for qualified privilege.

It should not be assumed that the full qualified privilege applies to stories of the excesses of every petty local committee, particularly when not germane to the public questions before it.

> ILLUSTRATION TO THE CONTRARY
> During (or possibly at a special conference after) a session of the city council, in response to questioning by a councilman, the city manager said he was not going to promote two police officers because they were insubordinate and should have been fired. The Passaic *Daily News* had a qualified privilege to publish the report.

The defamatory remarks pertained strictly to the conduct of the policemen while on duty—did not accuse either of a crime or attack them personally.

III. EXECUTIVE PROCEEDINGS

We are now examining the qualified privilege which protects repetition of libelous statements made in the course of executive—administrative—proceedings.

TOP LEVEL PROCEEDINGS

Fair reports of formal executive hearings of high order carry a privilege equivalent to that for reports of judicial or legislative proceedings. It is assumed that the hearings on this plateau:

> (i) are pursuant to statutory authority or inaugurated by an official of highest rank (usually the President, a cabinet officer or a governor, or the head of an important branch of government);

(ii) will be conducted with a certain formality and will appear to be keeping within an authorized sphere;

(iii) are open to the public;

and that:

(iv) protection somewhat analogous to that of a court proceeding is afforded the persons who are the subjects of the investigation and to witnesses; and that

(v) third parties who are defamed will be given an opportunity to clear their names if they so desire.

If these conditions are met, executive proceedings may be reported without tremor, as would a full-dress trial.

The problem arises so often that it may be worth while to restate the guidelines: When reporting the proceedings of an administrative committee, do not assume it to be an occasion of absolute privilege which assures the publisher of a secure occasion of qualified privilege if he accurately reports what was there said, *unless* the committee is clearly an orderly group, proceeding under (i) statutory authority, or (ii) at the direction of the President, a governor, cabinet officer, or other high executive acting within his sphere, or (iii) is constituted by an administrative board or body while performing functions authorized by law.

SECONDARY HEARINGS AND INVESTIGATIONS;
ADMINISTRATIVE PROCEEDINGS

As executive proceedings decline in dignity and public importance, it is necessary to be more alert than in the case of judicial proceedings in an established court. A court is a court, even though the judicial officer be a rural justice of the peace, unlearned in the law, perhaps not even authorized to practice law. Executive proceedings may grade down from a Warren Commission to quizzing by a petty official—perhaps with no statutory authorization to conduct the inquisition.

So executive hearings (administrative proceedings) must be considered on their merits. An inquiry by the mayor of a village does not enjoy the status equal to that of an extradition proceeding or a hearing incident to a proposed pardon or an investigation into important affairs of the commonwealth by or on behalf of a governor.

QUOTING PUBLIC STATEMENTS BY OFFICIALS

Public statements *by* important governmental officials are the subject of this section. Stories *about* public officials are covered in Part IV of this chapter, and editorials which castigate them in Chapter 8.

Statements by public officials fall into the three classes:

(i) those made in course of official duties and strictly limited to things germane to a problem within the jurisdiction of the official; *or*

(ii) in part devoted to matters of public concern and in part to defamatory digressions not important to the presentation of the public matters being discussed; *or*

(iii) with little or no ground for asserting that any of the statements are in the public weal.

A qualified privilege attends repetition of statements within class (i). Obviously libelous statements which are in class (iii) should not be repeated unless the publisher is prepared to prove substantial truth.

If the statement falls in class (ii), consummate care must be used before repeating a libel per se—was it a necessary or at least a proper part of the handling of a matter of public consequence within the orbit of this official or reporting to the public in respect thereto? Or was it part of the ramblings of a politician?

ILLUSTRATIONS:

1. The governor of Arkansas held a press conference and released a "Press Statement of Governor Faubus." The release dealt with irregularities in nursing homes and improper acts by nursing home proprietors. He characterized conditions as a "sordid and shocking story of mismanagement and misdeeds."

The *Gazette* sent a reporter to one of the homes to interview management. It published the governor's statement plus a denial of the charges by the home. The newspaper won the libel suit because of: (i) qualified privilege, the good faith demonstrated by the careful reporting and publication of the denials by the accused, and (ii) consent to publication given incident to the reporter's visit to the home and interview with plaintiff.

Note that plaintiff sued despite fair treatment and apparent consent.

2. The Scranton *Times* published an abridged report of an investigation made at the direction of Governor Averill Harriman of New York into the activities and associations of those known to have been at a meeting of underworld overlords and their vassals. The plaintiff was a delegate. The report mentioned an arrest on rape charges and association with racketeers in his biographical sketch.

The Supreme Court of Pennsylvania decided: (i) the governor of New York enjoyed absolute immunity when publishing the report; (ii) because it is in the public interest that information be made available as to what takes place in public affairs, the newspaper had a qualified privilege when it told of the report; (iii) the article as a whole was a fair and substantially correct summary of the governmental report; the qualified privilege had not been abused.

The points relied upon by the Pennsylvania court constitute a typical—a classic—design of the three cornerstones to privilege.

3. A director of the Internal Revenue Service issued a press release stating that assets of plaintiff had been seized

to satisfy delinquent income taxes. The *News-Journal* ran a story. The director misspoke. *Held*: The district director had either an absolute or qualified privilege as to the press release. Therefore, the newspaper had a qualified privilege when repeating it in good faith without knowledge of the falsity.

The district director was considered to be a policy-making official of the executive branch of government. His area of discretion included the drastic action he erroneously said was taken against a citizen.

Police, prosecuting attorneys, and other law enforcement officials have wide powers—a man may be charged with murder. Yet, as has been seen, more often than not, their public statements are devoid of privilege. Except when quoting a summit official, sound judgment must be used. Under one set of circumstances it would be safe—it might be a duty to the public—to quote an announcement by the chairman of the Port Commission. On another occasion the answer might be "no qualified privilege." Absent duty to the public; when secondary officials are the speakers, play safe. The essentials can be told sans libel.

RARE EXCEPTIONS

There is an occasional exception. It is libelous to say that a columnist or newscaster is a liar. The President of the United States calls one a liar on an occasion of no privilege under ordinary rules. Because of the eminence of the speaker, what he said may be repeated. But not so, if a congressman said the same when not on the floor of the House, unless it is possible to tie to another type of privilege.

The illustration just given does not warrant an inference that privileged statements stem only from top officials. But as the rank becomes lower, those who repeat the official defamation must use increasing care to make sure that it is made incident to official duties and is directly related to the performance of official functions.

QUOTING OFFICEHOLDERS AS CANDIDATES

When the public official who might be safely quoted as a public official performing the functions of his office becomes a candidate for re-election, other principles apply. The strict legal rule is that there is no qualified privilege when:

(i) perpetuating the defamations of a vicious or careless candidate by print or broadcast; or
(ii) publishing or repeating his ads or other written material.

Such should be assumed to be the law, except in important situations where the officeholder seeks to oust another—a legislator runs for governor—a greater latitude might be allowed in view of the *New York Times* decision discussed in Part IV of this chapter.

When checking the accuracy of news stories a reporter may be held to a higher standard of performance than is expectable of a candidate for elective office when—in the heat of the campaign—he assembles material for campaign propaganda.

SPOT NEWS

Situations can occur when spot news—in contrast to ads—may, almost must, be published even though libelous, because of the importance of the candidate and the occasion of the utterance. At the apex would be a President or a governor seeking re-election. His libel is an ad-lib uttered during a television interview. Millions hear it. As a practical matter, he will be quoted by most news media. Similar considerations apply to spot news reporting a vicious attack on a high official by the rival candidate.

Grading down to tertiary offices where a libel should not be repeated, no matter how newsworthy, a rule of reason may be applied by management in telling what officeholders as candidates have actually said on important occasions. These comments do not apply to what their followers say, unless the speaker is of great eminence and the news story almost inescapable.

There are lowly considerations which may have a bearing when weighing the risk. To illustrate: It may be safer to publish the story of a libel about the winning candidate than the man destined to defeat. If the defamed candidate is elected, it is most unlikely that he will sue a publisher who has given him fair coverage. Certainly not if the publisher has happened to support him editorially and has given him favorable publicity. He will want continued support.

But what if the candidate is defeated by a narrow margin and the libel per se was circulated or broadcast shortly before election day? Truth may be the only defense. The judge should instruct the jury that no special damages may be allowed for the defeat on election day. That pleasant sounding instruction may prove to be of little or no aid to the defendant. There being a libel per se, the jury may bring in a verdict sufficient to buy a press or rebuild the tower, unless truth has been proved.

The statutory responsibilities of radio and television in respect to political broadcasts are delineated in Chapter 15.

IV. WHEN A PUBLIC OFFICIAL IS DEFAMED;
CANDIDATES; SUNDRY SITUATIONS

Rules that govern the people's right to know what goes on in public affairs have been changing.

Departing from the traditional strict rule requiring proof of truth, courts began to recognize that it is no longer realistic to assume that even the largest publisher or broadcaster has personnel sufficient to investigate every facet of public affairs and to be able to prove that every statement that touches the administration of government is true.

In response to the public's need to know what is happening in government, a general rule began to evolve, to the effect that if the publisher in good faith believes the statement to be true, has made a fair investigation or has received his news in the belief that a fair investigation has been made, and publishes or broadcasts in good faith, without malice, there is a qualified privilege. As stated by the Supreme Court of West Virginia:

> . . . a citizen of a free state having an interest in the conduct of the affairs of his government should not be held to strict accountability for a misstatement of fact, if he has tried to ascertain the truth and, on a reasonable basis, honestly and in good faith believes that the statements made by him are true.

Dismissing a libel suit brought by a congressman based upon a newspaper article charging him with anti-Semitism, an eminent federal judge said:

> Cases which impose liability for erroneous reports of the political conduct of officials reflect the obsolete doctrine that the governed must not criticize their governors. . . . The protection of the public requires not merely discussion, but information. . . . Errors of fact, particularly in regard to a man's mental state and processes, are inevitable.

Such was the direction of the law. But it could not be said to be the law generally until the *New York Times* decision by the United States Supreme Court.

Public Officials

The *Times* published an ad which described the maltreatment of Negro students protesting segregation, bombings, and other disgraceful conduct in Montgomery, Alabama. Certain of the factual statements were clearly libelous per se. Some were false statements. Were they privileged?

The court made its decision against the background of a profound national commitment to the principle that debate on public issues should be uninhibited and robust and that it may well include vehement, caustic, and sometimes unpleasantly sharp attacks on government and public officials.

The ad was an expression of grievance and protest on a major public issue. The question was whether the falsities forfeited the freedom of expression upon public questions secured by the Constitution.

Recognizing that erroneous statement is inevitable in free debate, the court held that the constitutional guaranty of freedom of speech and press affords a publisher a qualified privilege of honest mistake when discussing public questions. Public men are, as it were, public property.

Before the official may recover damages for a defamatory falsehood *relating to his official conduct* he must prove that the statement was made with actual malice—that is, with knowledge that it was false or with reckless disregard of whether or not it was false.

Development of the Rule

Soon after the *Times* decision, in a libel case brought against the *New York Daily News,* the United States Court of Appeals forecast the development of the rule.

Although the public official is the strongest case for the

constitutional compulsion of such a privilege, it is questionable whether in principle the decision can be so limited. A candidate for public office would seem an inevitable candidate for extension. . . . Once that extension [is] made, the participant in public debate on an issue of grave public concern would be next in line.

Subsequent cases properly extend the rule to include false reports of important matters of public importance. In each of the following applications of the *Times* rule the article was held privileged although defamatory and although the facts stated were untrue, or presumed untrue for the purpose of the opinion:

1. A newspaper published a syndicated article about a congressman without attempting to verify the facts.
2. A wire service sent out a story concerning a private citizen involved in a civil riot. The newspaper did not check the facts.
3. A story in a student newspaper about a member of the student senate.
4. The General Walker stories—a public personage.
5. Unsanitary conditions in a food store based on erroneous report of health officers.
6. Statements by a mayor about an opponent made the day before election.
7. A seller of obscene books came within the rule when a radio station reported his arrest. The fact that he was not a public figure was held immaterial since he was involved in an event of public interest.

Persons already held within the rule include: the captain in a sheriff's office; the chairman of a political party board; a member of a school board and of a water district board; a judge running for office; a labor leader; and, in a rare situation where there is a grave public interest, a business executive. But he who publishes a libel, relying on the shield of "public concern," must be cautious and sincere.

As has been observed when reckoning the strength of a middling qualified privilege, the importance of the event may be considered. The conduct of a colonel would usually give rise to no more than a faint privilege. If he were in command of troops brought in to quell plundering after a flood, his activities might be subject to detailed scrutiny, and if libel were to slip in there would be a qualified privilege. But neighborhood interest is not enough. There must be a widespread public interest in a matter of consequence to government or the welfare of the people, and the challenged statement must be related to the public weal.

Material libelous per se should not be published in *sole* reliance upon the importance of the event without deliberate assumption of the risk by management. There may be another privilege to which to tie.

RECALL AND OTHER PETITIONS

Assertions of a recall petition not directed to efficiency or competency in office but to the officeholder's private life or honesty carry no privilege. If the story adheres to the language of a bona fide petition directed to conduct in public office, it is qualifiedly privileged.

But if the story goes beyond the petition, the publisher may be put to prove the truth of the libel. There should be no implication of guilt beyond the precise language of the petition.

These comments apply to other official petitions—recognized by statute—in respect to public affairs.

REPLIES TO ATTACKS

One who has been attacked by another has the right of self-defense. The role of publishers in such a situation is discussed in Chapter 9. When there is a broadcast by a political candidate, this right is in black and white under FCC regulations, as will be noted in Chapter 15.

SEMIPUBLIC PROCEEDINGS

Unless, because of unusual circumstances, the matter is of paramount public importance, there is no privilege when reporting private gatherings—church, society, lodge, stockholders' meetings, conventions, caucuses, community clubs, and the like. Political meetings afford no privilege, except in particular cases when the public interest justifies it.

There are exceptions. For example, an ecclesiastical trial may occur before a tribunal duly constituted by church law. If the proceeding is open to the public and is a matter of public importance, there may be a qualified privilege. But all factors should be weighed.

When the legislature has given a medical or bar association or other semipublic body authority in respect to admission and discipline, its public proceedings may carry a certain privilege.

LABOR DISPUTES

Labor disputes range from private dueling with no qualified privilege when publishing the recriminations of the warring factions, to major battles affecting everyone. The halting of transportation, a shut-down of essential utilities, the closing of hospitals, and many other casualties cannot be minimized nor can they be described without quotations from spokesmen for each side. Sometimes there is a clear privilege when quoting a public official speaking in line of duty. More often it is a question of sound practical judgment in the framework of public interest and necessity.

ILLUSTRATION

A newspaper published a letter from the union to employers. It announced the commencement of picketing. The article commented that: (i) the letter threatened "blackmail picketing," and (ii) would be used as a "gangster gun"; and (iii) the union did not care for the desires or rights of employees. The Supreme Court of Kansas held that *under the circumstances* there was no libel per se.

"Under the circumstances" means criteria to be considered by management when forecasting whether publication will be privileged.

INNOCENT THIRD PARTIES

Caveats (warnings) have already been given in respect to thoughtlessly naming innocent third parties. As the quality of the occasion of qualified privilege declines from the strongest occasions—typically, legislative proceedings—to the weaker—for example, a minor committee hearing—it becomes even more important to guard against libeling innocent third parties not in any way participants in those less significant proceedings.

V. LOSS OF PRIVILEGE; WEIGHING THE RISK

Two dozen occasions of qualified privilege have been described. They range from solid privileges (e.g., reporting a trial) to frail occasions, such as a press release by a county commissioner. One must be either clumsy or negligent to lose the former. The preservation of the latter is to the credit of an informed and alert staff.

The rule of the *Times* case, alone or as construed in the *Daily News* decision, is not a license for thoughtless handling of articles concerning officials, candidates, and others on a public forum. The challenged libel must (i) relate to official conduct, and (ii) be made without actual malice. If there is knowledge of the falsity or a reckless disregard of truth or falsity, a court or jury may find actual malice. These are factual questions; they may be submitted to an antagonistic jury.

Certainly if the reporter, rewrite man, broadcaster, or editor on duty knew of the falsity, that knowledge would be imputed to the publisher. What if one of them should have been alerted to possible falsity by facts or even rumors within his knowledge, yet he did not double check? Perhaps the records in the publisher's library prove falsity, yet they were not examined. A jury may find this a reckless disregard of truth. Illustrations abound.

There is the constant hazard that antagonists may attack each other in respect to matters not germane to public office or affairs. Such libels are not within the privilege. It is a fair forecast that within the next decade damages will be amerced against publishers whose personnel have overreached in reliance on the *Times* decision.

Identifying the Occasion or Person

In Chapter 5 it was remarked that when a source is quoted it should be identified. Whenever privilege is present, the nature of that privilege should be revealed in the publication or broadcast so that all will know the origin of the assertions.

Illustration

Secret Service men were quoted as charging Hughes and wife with making and passing bogus money. The article itself neither mentioned the Secretary of the Treasury nor intimated that it was reporting an official statement by him. When sued, the newspaper attributed the announcement to the Secretary of the Treasury.

The court held that undisclosed similarity or coincidence between a defendant's libelous statement and a public official's previous announcement is not enough to make the statement a report of the official announcement.

In the above illustration the court did not decide whether qualified privilege would extend to the report of such an "announcement" by the Secretary of the Treasury. If he speaks within the outer periphery of his official functions, he may be safely quoted. Suppose a deputy rather than a cabinet officer made the announcement. Whether he should charge named persons (presumably innocent) with passing bad checks is questionable. That is within the jurisdiction of law enforcement officers. It must always be remembered that the accused may be found "not guilty." The safer course would be to withhold names until a specific charge is in the records of the court.

ABUSE OF PRIVILEGE

If a qualified privilege is misused, it may be destroyed and lost as a defense. Privileges are not self-executing.

The fact that the story tells of a privileged occasion is not in itself enough. It must be consistent with the purposes of the qualified privilege. It must be an impartial (historical) account of the privileged event which included the defamation. The story may be lively, even sensational, but it must not distort. It must not be inaccurate, inflammatory, vicious, or malicious when reciting the defamatory statements made in the course of a privileged event.

In respect to accuracy, media are not held to the scientific precision demanded in, for example, technical reporting. It is enough if the article gives a substantially correct account of what happened.

WHEN PRIVILEGE IS WEAK

When the occasion is not clearly one that affords a reliable qualified privilege, the publisher's position is strengthened by including statements from the person defamed. These should be given a prominence similar to the charges against him. Even the sentence "John Doe could not be reached for comment" helps somewhat. It shows a desire to give an impartial account.

WEIGHING THE RISK

Words and circumstances are infinite in number and character. Permissible stories cannot be catalogued. Often the degree (amount) of protection actually afforded by an occasion of qualified privilege cannot be estimated without precise knowledge of the occasion which is believed to create the privilege to repeat.

Editorial and managerial discretion must be used, taking into consideration:

(i) the importance to the public of the subject under discussion;
(ii) the eminence of the public officer or the nature of the public proceeding;
(iii) the circumstances of the utterance;
(iv) the *provable* reputation of the person defamed;
(v) whether because of other relevant and provable offenses he is in any position to bring suit against the publisher; and
(vi) all other facts and circumstances.

The expression "other relevant and provable offenses" needs illustration. Here is an actual sequence, typical of a situation when it can be proved that the accused did do something else just as bad which is sufficiently related to the story in question:

A reputable husband was suspected of murdering his second wife. The first stories were written warily. Suddenly the body was found, and he made an easily provable confession. The field became wide open—headlines announced, "Husband Confesses Murder." Then he was suspected of having murdered his first wife. This he hotly denied. His denials mentioned third persons, connecting them with the disappearance of his first wife. As to the husband, the easily provable confession in respect to wife number two made safe enough the publication or broadcast of the details of the investigation of the death of wife number one.* But prudence indicated utmost caution concerning the third persons mentioned by Bluebeard.

A REVIEW

Affairs public proliferate. More and more events occur in the twilight zones of privilege. A partial review may be useful.

The cautious course is to assume that only those statements of a public official that are clearly within the orbit of his duties may be repeated with confidence that the repetition is secure behind the barrier of qualified privilege. A presidential press conference is not an official proceeding. Yet surely any statement on public affairs thus openly made by the President of the United States can be safely passed along.

But (except as the rule of the *Times* decision is extended) there would be no recognized *legal* privilege in repeating defamatory attacks upon his opponent made by this same man while campaigning for re-election. Again, as a practical matter, whatever he said would probably be published.

Unofficial statements by lesser personages grade down to zero as far as privilege to repeat is concerned. In a matter of great public importance, the statement of the mayor of New York, speaking as mayor and not as a politician, might be repeated with confidence that, as a practical matter, there is a certain protection—a sort of extralegal practical privilege—if true qualified privilege fails. The utterances of a small town mayor or chairman of an irrigation district would have no such additional extralegal sanctity.

Similarly, there is, by legal rule, a most vigorous qualified

* Whether such details should be published is a subject considered in Chapter 16—"Free Speech—Fair Trial."

privilege in telling of legislative proceedings. But in practice the courts and juries will not grant the same protection when reporting the antics of a meeting of county commissioners as when reporting the deliberations of the Senate of the United States. As to the former, a court or jury may more quickly find an abuse of privilege, whatever the legal theories may be.

The practical result is that statements made before a city council, for instance, cannot always be repeated with the same confidence in a shield of privilege as statements made on the floor of the Congress or a state legislature.

In Part I, Chapter 6, under the heading Administrative Proceedings, note was made of an SEC hearing which lacked certain attributes of a proceeding which carries an absolute privilege. A witness at that hearing was held liable for his slanders. Would the repetition of the testimony (via broadcast or print, making it a libel) be protected by a qualified privilege? Probably not, unless the overriding public importance of the subject or the witness makes the news account a public duty—to be performed with utmost caution.

Whenever an occasion is deficient in factors assuring absolute privilege, libelous statements not strictly germane to the public question involved should be eschewed, and even if relevant, should be repeated cautiously, making sure that the person defamed has an opportunity to give his version of the story.

CHAPTER 8

COMMENT AND CRITICISM

It is much easier to be critical than to be correct.

DISRAELI

THE defense of qualified privilege applies to defamatory statements of fact. The defense of fair comment (sometimes called
privileged criticism) applies to defamatory comments. The
one permits factual statements; the other permits expressions of opinion which otherwise would cause actionable
damage.

Fact and comment do not dwell in sharply divided compart-
ments. They mingle in the same speech or editorial—frequently
in the same paragraph. Not unnaturally, court decisions sometimes treat the two as almost alike. Nevertheless, there are
important distinctions between qualified privilege and fair comment. The essence may be stated thus:

> A certain false assertion of fact would be an actionable
> libel were it not for the qualified privilege in saying or re-
> peating this libelous thing.
> Fair comment is an opinion fairly stated in relation to the
> facts. It is no libel.

In short: One is a libel against which there is a defense; the other is not a libel.

I. Who May Be Criticized

Natural subjects of criticism and adverse comment include public officials (judges, legislators, and executives); candidates for public office; public institutions; matters of public concern (including the work of independent contractors being paid out of public funds); scientific, artistic, literary works; dramatic productions and exhibitions; and sporting events catering to the public.

Groups dedicated, in whole or in part, to influencing public opinion or changing the laws or customs of the land—from a manufacturers' association to a labor union and from the Ku Klux Klan to CORE—are subject to comment and criticism.

An organization which publicly solicits funds for the support of its activities should expect the white light of inquiry and comment. The same may be said of an individual who enters the public arena, though not a candidate.

It has been emphasized that the degree—the quality—of qualified privilege varies with the occasion—for instance, a United States senator vis-à-vis a deputy sheriff.

In similar fashion the freedom to criticize varies with the subject of the criticism. The shield is strongest when criticizing public officials. So officeholders will be first considered, and then candidates. The discussion in the opening paragraphs of Part IV of Chapter 7 applies to comment as well as to news reports.

Public Officials—The Strict Rule

The traditional rule (once sound, but by changed conditions rendered harsh and now outmoded by the *Times* decision) is that the comment is fair when:

1. *It is based on facts provably true.*
2. It is free of imputations of corrupt or dishonorable motives on the part of the person who is criticized except insofar as such imputations are warranted by the facts.
3. It is an honest expression of opinion—the motive is the public weal, not desire to harm.

This must be remembered as the background when, shortly, we look at the limitations of the new liberal rule.

Proving the truth of the facts upon which the comment is based was not too heavy a burden—was not against the public interest—when the rule evolved. When matters of public import were fewer and less complicated, when it was expectable that the facts behind honest criticism would be known in the sense of being provable, there could be little suppression of comment by a rule requiring proof of truth.

Now, as suggested in the discussion of qualified privilege, government has become exceedingly big and complex. Unless publishers have latitude for factual error when in good faith, without malice, they criticize public officials, necessary criticism will be stifled.

THE MARCH TOWARD REALITY

Responsive to these changed conditions (even before the *Times* decision, and based on the factors just indicated rather than the federal Constitution), a more liberal rule has been supplanting the old. Under this more realistic rule, a misstatement of fact about a public official or candidate, in connection with matters of public concern, is privileged. Hence, there is a defense to the libel action if the statement is made for the benefit of the public, in the absence of malice, and in the honest belief that it is true. As indicated, "honest belief" presupposes care in gathering the news or receipt from a reliable source.

PUBLIC OFFICIALS—THE RIGHT RULE

The ad before the court in the *New York Times* case was mixed fact and criticism. Privilege for the citizen—critic of officialdom—was sanctified. "It is as much his duty to criticize as it is the official's duty to administer." The rule now is that, since the Constitution requires recognition of the conditional privilege for honest misstatement of fact, it follows that a defense of fair comment will shield an honest expression of opinion based either on true or privileged statements of fact. Both defenses, of course, fail if the public official proves actual malice, which a jury may pin upon the publisher even though the defense thinks the plaintiff has failed to prove it.

When criticizing a public official the writer of the editorial should:

   (i) know or in good faith believe the facts to be true; assume that a suspicion of factual untruth amounts to a reckless disregard of truth;

  (ii) double check if there is a factual libel, the accuracy of which can be checked without disproportionate expense or delay;

 (iii) criticize in good faith—for the public good;

 (iv) keep his criticism in the groove—official acts and affairs; qualifications for office—stay away from personal life unless clearly germane to the public affairs under discussion.

CRITICISM OF CANDIDATES

In discussions of candidates, the privilege should be the same as when a person already in office is the target. But do not yet assume that it is. Be more careful. Apply the foregoing caveats with greater severity.

CRITICISM OF EVENTS OF GREAT PUBLIC IMPORTANCE

Here again we have a logical extension of the rule of the *New York Times* opinion. It is a step beyond candidates and two steps beyond the decision itself.

When discussing factual privilege in connection with events of paramount public importance, we suggested that the trend toward broadening privilege in public affairs may be considered by management when weighing the risk of publication. An operating rule should not yet be assumed.

CRITICISM OF PRIVATE VENTURES

Some private ventures are clearly in the public domain, others not. It must *not* be assumed that the strengthening privilege in respect to comment on public affairs extends to private affairs. Indeed, in Chapter 13 it will be seen that the right of privacy is being protected and extended.

When a person in private life is the target and the subject matter is personal, the facts on which criticism is based must be provably true.

CRITICISM OF THE COURT

When the comments or story indicate mishandling of a judicial proceeding, there are three elements to consider: (i) possible contempt of court; (ii) the chance that excessive zeal on the part of the reporter or other inaccuracy has resulted in an abuse of the qualified privilege and consequent vulnerability to libel actions by counsel, litigants, witnesses, or third parties mentioned in the trial; and (iii) possible libel of the judge.

The judges realize that they are not "set on a pedestal and decorated with a halo." They recognize that judicial conduct should be an object of "constant watchfulness . . . and its judgments subject to the freest criticism."

Referring to human frailties and fallibilities, Mr. Justice Felix Frankfurter remarked that: ". . . judges must be kept mindful of their limitations and of their ultimate public responsibility by a vigorous stream of criticism expressed with candor however blunt." Speaking for the United States Supreme Court, Mr. Justice Hugo L. Black said: "And an enforced silence, . . . would probably engender resentment, suspicion, and contempt much more than it would enhance respect."

Often the most pungent critics of the opinions of a court are members of that very court. "This case is a shocking abuse of judicial authority. It is without precedent in the books," three judges recently wrote.

The severest criticism, well timed and properly expressed— that does not impinge upon a pending suit—is not a contempt of court. Nor will a judge as an individual have a cause of action based on defamation.

II. Criticism May Be Severe

Once established as proper, criticism may be powerful. Subject to the rules already discussed, the critic can write a philippic. He may condemn in no uncertain terms. He may use satire and proper invective, flanked by a cartoon.

Dismissing a complaint by Lord Tilkin that one of Lord Beaverbrook's newspapers had been overly rough, the Queen's Bench Division ruled:

> Any person is entitled to say, by way of comment on a matter of public interest, what he honestly thinks, however exaggerated, obstinate or prejudiced it may be. Such comment is fair and sustainable as a defense to a libel action unless it is so strong that no fair-minded person could have made it honestly.

Summing up, His Worship warned: "You should not misstate the material facts upon which you are commenting."

A book, for example, may be referred to as dull, shallow, and stupid, if the reviewer so believes. However, the review will not be protected as a fair criticism if the author is accused of plagiarism; that charge must be proved true.

Performers and musicians can be verbally crucified in respect to artistic competence, but not otherwise.

It should not be intimated that an athlete deliberately failed to do his utmost to win. Hints of pay-offs or deals should be eschewed, unless the publisher is prepared to prove the truth or the announcement was made on an occasion of privilege.

In the gray area where it is unclear whether a certain organization or person is a proper subject of criticism, the criticism itself should be restrained and constructive, and the facts provably true.

A Checklist for Criticism

If there is a negative answer to any one of the following six questions, the proposed criticism should be reviewed again with possible libel especially in mind:

1. Is the subject of public interest or concern?
2. Are the facts upon which the criticism is based provably true or, in the alternative, clearly under the rule pertaining to public officials?
3. Are the circumstances—including publisher's resources and situation—such that the jury might well decide that failure to check the facts demonstrates malice or cavalier disregard of the truth?
4. Is there an expression of opinion in contrast to an assertion of fact?
5. Is it a fair comment?
6. Is it in the public interest, free from the taint of malice?

Libel based on comment or criticism almost always originates in a situation that could easily be avoided by use of moderate journalistic skills. There is usually at least a little time for reflection and verification—the deadline is not ten minutes away. With care, stringent and caustic comment and criticism may be made almost wholly safe—not safe from many threats of suit by disgruntled politicians and from occasional actual nuisance suits—but safe from verdicts in significant sums. The editorial that smacks of libel should be read to counsel.

Ad-Lib Disc Jockeys

The ad-lib radio and television broadcasts (including "personality-type" disc jockeys who intersperse recordings with comments upon the world and life in general) pose peculiar problems. There is little or no opportunity to check such remarks beforehand. Disc jockeys and all other ad-libbers must be schooled to keep their remarks within the rules of fair comment and criticism. Shop-talk programs are of the same class.

Libel of Government

Government as such, as a massive apparatus, cannot be libeled. Strictures against "the Congress" or "the Army" or the "bureaucrats of the Agricultural Department" are too general to give anyone a cause of action.

The danger zone is reached when the editorial attacks a small governmental entity (school district, for instance) or a department of government under circumstances where an employee or official is able to demonstrate that, though unnamed, he has been identified.[*] If so, the defenses of privilege and comment will be available as when attacking public officials.

[*] This is treated in Chapter 4 under the heading "Libel by Reference to a Class."

MULTIPLE CRITIQUES

It will be stressed that when there are several barbs and truth is the defense, substantial truth must be proved as to each. Similarly, if there is more than one criticism—whether different points or phraseology—the propriety of the criticism must be proved as to each.

ILLUSTRATION

Plaintiff owned a private dock. By newspaper ads and otherwise he attempted to influence the city council and the public against construction of a competitive dock. By injecting himself into a matter of public concern and criticizing public officials, plaintiff invited comment and criticism leveled at him. Six alleged libels were brushed aside by the Supreme Court of Iowa. But the *Evening Democrat* let down its guard on the seventh.

It said: "There is no honorable reason for opposing a local boat harbor." The writer forgot that the antonym of "honorable" is dishonorable, shameful, unjust. Here the newspaper abused and (as treated by the court) lost its qualified privilege.

Though the court speaks of qualified privilege, this was a fair comment case where the newspaper made an unjustified criticism rather than a factual statement.

LOSS OF RIGHT—A REVIEW

The necessity of free and forceful comment, despite the hazards, is so great that a rephrasing of basic principles seems justified. The essentials of fairness are lacking in the following instances:

1. If the comment assaults motive, conduct, or character unrelated to the public matters to which the comment really relates.
2. If it criticizes a person's private life in respect to affairs

unrelated to the public matter properly under discussion.

3. If it accuses a person of a crime or employs degrading or insulting epithets, except (i) when necessary or proper to show his unfitness for, or unfaithfulness in, public office, or (ii) when otherwise clearly appropriate to a legitimate end sought by a comment made in the public interest.

4. If the criticism is malicious—and a jury may infer malice from conduct.

It must be remembered that public policy does not require the protection of a person who, instead of expressing his honest opinion, seizes upon an opportunity to gratify his own malice or to exhibit his skill in vituperative utterance.

CRITICISM REVERSED

A news broadcaster, or commentator assumes a dual role of private citizen and public figure. While not an elected public official (an Ohio court remarked), his position must be considered analogous as far as criticism of his programs is concerned. His broadcasts are tantamount to a production or performance for public exhibition. Hence he submits them to criticism within the rules pertaining to fair comment. The same may, of course, be said in respect to all writers whose views are widely circulated.

CHAPTER 9

TRUTH, CONSENT, AND REPLIES

> *Nothing is so firmly believed as what we least know.*
>
> MONTAIGNE

PROOF that the defamatory statement is substantially true is a complete defense to a civil action of libel.* "Justification" is a plea of truth.

TRUTH

A reporter may "know" many things which he could not possibly prove in court. Hearsay and gossip are not admissible in evidence, even though everybody "knows" the statements to be true. *A defamatory article should be presumed false unless it can be proved true by evidence which is admissible in court*

---

* Except in those few states, such as Illinois and Massachusetts, that do not accept truth as a complete defense if the publication was from "malicious motives" or was "motivated by actual malice" or which require that along with truth it must be shown the publication was for "justifiable ends" or related to a "subject of public concern."

and which will be available for the trial. It should not be published unless it is (i) provably true, or it is (ii) believed to be true and is clearly within the rules of qualified privilege or fair comment.

ILLUSTRATION

At a political gathering a candidate for public office shouts that his rival obtained his naturalization papers through perjury. It is easily provable that the story quotes the speaker accurately. But to sustain a defense of truth in an action brought by the rival, the publisher or broadcaster must go further and prove the perjury.

A mistaken belief in the truth of the matter published, although honest and reasonable, is not a defense unless the publication was privileged.

Fortunately, it is not necessary to prove that a story is meticulously true. Slight inaccuracies of expression are immaterial provided that the defamatory charge is true in substance.

MULTIPLE BARBS

Substantial truth must be proved in respect to each and every separate libel—every sting—in the publication. Otherwise a plea of truth (justification) fails as a complete defense. Then—possibly before a hostile jury under instructions from the judge—defense counsel will be confined to the contention that after all it was but a little libel. Yet if this little residuary libel is a libel per se, the jurymen can price it about as they please.

CONSENT

A person who consents to the publication cannot recover. As in the case of truth, consent means a consent which can be proved at the trial. The consent must be to the type of publication in question. If Joe College, class of '55, consents to the publication of a caricature and a supposedly humorous but scurrilous story in his fraternity magazine, he has not consented to a reprint in a publication of general circulation.

PSEUDO CONSENTS

Sometimes a person defamed in a proposed story readily grants an interview giving his version of the affair. *This does not in itself constitute a consent to publication of the defamation.* But, if he does not object to publication of the entire account as read to him, the interview is a significant factor when deciding whether as a practical matter the story, including his statements, may be run.

REPLIES TO ATTACKS

As between adversaries in the public forum, there is a considerable right of self-defense. When an individual has been attacked by, say, a political opponent, he may wish to reply through the medium which carried the original attack. Hence, even though the reply is defamatory of the original attacker, a broadcaster or publisher may have a qualified privilege in disseminating the reply, if the new defamatory matter is essential to support a contention that the first attack was unjustified.

Because the libelous reply is usually in response to a libelous accusation, the publisher or broadcaster could be in the midst of one libel already uttered and another potential. If he refuses to pass along the reply to the public, the injured party will claim connivance and malice. But if the reply is beyond what is necessary to answer the original attack, the originator will wail. The statutory position of the broadcaster of political material is considered in Chapter 15.

A danger is that the retort may not be responsive to the attack or might be stronger than is proper. Ordinarily, one may not shoot to kill an unarmed man when the present danger is no more than fisticuffs.

ILLUSTRATIONS

1. The plaintiff accused certain stockholders of a corporation of mismanagement and questioned their honesty. The reply called plaintiff a "shady" lawyer who kept clients' money and said that his future status as a lawyer was in doubt. This was an irrelevant attack on plaintiff personally; the reply was not privileged.

2. The *Minneapolis Tribune* ran a story imputing malpractice to the plaintiff doctor. The defendant newspaper pleaded that it was replying to a libelous article run the day before in another paper at the instance of plaintiff; it admitted the response was made in a moment of anger over the first publication. Because, as the court put it, there was time for "blood to cool," the first libel was not a defense to the libelous reply.

3. *Colliers* magazine accused a food processing company of intentionally conducting a false advertising campaign. The food company fought back by saying that the magazine had prostituted the truth in its columns in an effort to force advertisers to buy space. A New York court found the reply responsive to the defamation by *Colliers*.

In some states remedial legislation may be an aid in defending suits stemming from replies to attacks.

CHAPTER 10

CORRECTIONS AND RETRACTIONS

> *Confession of our faults is the next thing to innocency.*
>
> PUBLILIUS SYRUS

THE importance of giving an accused person an opportunity to state his side in a story when it is first published or broadcast is emphasized elsewhere. Such an explanation may keep alive a qualified privilege which otherwise might be lost; it shows a desire to be fair and rebuts malice. Situations where falsity is claimed or suspected in a story already broadcast or published are somewhat different.

MITIGATION OF DAMAGES

Whether a correction or retraction should be made is a neat question of policy, depending upon all the circumstances and upon the law of the state where suit will be brought. About half the states have adopted statutes to the effect that a retraction may be introduced in evidence in mitigation of damages. A number of states limit recovery to actual provable damage unless a retraction is demanded and refused.

Other legislative safeguards to news media require that if he seeks general damages, plaintiff must plead and prove (i) that there was an intent to defame, or (ii) in the absence of such an intent, failure to retract upon written demand made within a specified time.

Statutory requirements vary. If publishing (communicating) in a state which enjoys legislation of this character, media should have detailed instructions from local counsel as to procedures to be followed.

UNDERCUTTING THE DEFENSE OF TRUTH

If the principal justification is truth, a retraction may amount to an admission of falsity in circumstances where, if the admission had not been made, the defendant would have been able to prove substantial truth.

Insurance policies sometimes require the publisher to correct or retract the statement which is attacked as false and libelous. Occasionally they say "immediately." The insured must choose between (i) ignoring the terms of his policy, or (ii) hypocritically conceding that something is false though he still believes it to be true. The provision should be to this effect:

> If and when the Assured is informed that any person asserts that a false and libelous publication has been made concerning him (or her or it, as the case may be) the Assured will promptly investigate the claim and if (in the best judgment of the Assured and its counsel, if consulted) a retraction is in order, Assured will promptly publish whatever retraction or correction then seems appropriate in the situation.

The above is not an unfair or undue burden upon the carrier. It may save payment of a claim which probably would be pressed if falsity were admitted.

Effect of Refusal

Refusal to correct or retract a defamatory statement may be used to show malice or a callous disregard for the rights of others. Hence, if truth is not one of the principal defenses, a full and prompt correction or retraction is usually the better policy, although it is recognized that neither will ordinarily create a complete defense.

Be Gracious

If a correction or retraction is in order, it should not be grudgingly or ambiguously made. It should be full and frank, though it need not be abject. If printed, it should be published in as conspicuous a place as the article complained of. If the retraction is over the air, and is incident to a serious libel which has attracted attention, some effort should be made to assure a listening audience greater than that which heard the broadcast. If possible, a rating should be made so that evidence tending to prove the number who listened to the correction will be available if needed.

A Practical Hint

Sometimes, *by agreement,* an affirmative story which makes no reference to the libel is a better solace to the aggrieved. *To illustrate:* The publication or broadcast defamed Jones by saying he was involved in a fraud. It may be possible to prove the story true; but that is not certain. Jones threatens suit for libel. If he, too, is not sure of his case, a pleasant story telling of his fine work in the Elks Lodge or of his daughter's wedding may satisfy him—without putting the publisher in an untenable position.

CHAPTER 11

CONTEMPTS OF COURT

If all printers were determin'd not to print any thing till they were sure it would offend no body, there would be very little printed.

BENJAMIN FRANKLIN

THE First Amendment to the Constitution of the United States says that "Congress shall make no law . . . abridging the freedom of speech, or of the press . . ."—guarantees against transgression of freedom of speech and of the press, now, of course, including other media.

The Fifth Amendment to the federal Constitution provides that "No person shall . . . be deprived of life, liberty, or property, without due process of law . . ."—guarantees of due process—a fair trial.

The Sixth assures an accused "a speedy and public trial by an impartial jury." A public trial is a guarantee *to the accused* that he will be fairly dealt with and not unjustly condemned. History shows that secret trials are effective instruments of oppression.

Whether or not a state constitution has similar provisions, the Fourteenth Amendment, as now construed, makes these fundamentals (due process—public trial) applicable to state courts.

A public trial, then, is an ingredient of a fair trial. It becomes truly public because of news media, not by word of mouth originating with (usually) the handful who heard the trial. Nevertheless, the courts limit what newsmen may deem full coverage of a matter of public consequence.

THE CONFLICT

Freedom of the press and fair trial are not in themselves the ends. Both are necessary adjuncts to the goal of freedom for the individual. Yet at times license to report court proceedings seems to clash with the judicial concept of a fair trial. The advent of photography and television accentuates the problem. The presence of reporters is accepted as a matter of course except for a few hearings which, as a matter of public policy, are conducted privately. Reporters sit quietly with pad and pencil.

Cameras and television equipment introduce a new element. Litigants, witnesses, lawyers, and even the judge himself may be camera-conscious or camera-shy. Many jurists believe that photographic activities within the courtroom make a fair trial difficult, if not impossible.

RIGHTS AND RESPONSIBILITIES

Affirmative aspects of freedom of the press and freedom of speech are reflected in qualified privilege and the right of fair comment and criticism. Every right carries a corollary duty. The constitutional guarantees of free speech and a free press are expressly or implicitly subject to the burden that the speaker may be responsible for an abuse of his freedom. One manifestation of that responsibility is found in the law of libel; another in the right of privacy. A third segment is found in the rules pertaining to contempt of court.

This chapter has to do with traditional contempts of court. Chapter 16 is dedicated to an overlapping but wider problem— the achievement of a reconciliation between the essentials of a fair trial and freedom to report to the public what goes on before, during, and after a trial.

CONTEMPT OF COURT

Any act which significantly derogates the dignity and authority of the court or which tends to impede or frustrate the administration of justice may be a contempt of court. The power to punish for contempt is inherent in the courts. This is deemed essential to the preservation of an independent judiciary and the protection of litigants.

As reflected in Chapter 8, the courts have no immunity from criticism. Under the rules there reviewed, anyone has wide latitude in honest though severe editorial comment upon the courts. Judicial inefficiency may be exposed. But a story or photo which tends (i) to produce an atmosphere of prejudice where a pending case is being or is to be tried; (ii) to delay or interfere with the administration of justice; or (iii) to cause justice to miscarry, may be held to be in contempt of court.

A case on trial is not an essential ingredient. Criticism of the law enforcement plans of an imperious judge, with "an excellent example of shotgun justice" as the punch line, resulted in a contempt citation to the editor and the posting of a $50,000 bond to avoid immediate commitment to the bastille.

TYPICAL CONTEMPTS

Critical editorial comment ineptly worded in respect to a pending suit is an obvious path to contempt proceedings. Perhaps the most frequent offense is playing up the opinions of detectives, alienists, and other experts, thus prejudicing a community and prospective jurors in advance of trial. While the case is being tried, publication of supposed facts not admissible in evidence may force the judge to grant a mistrial—here clearly interfering with the administration of justice. This may be so even though the jury is held overnight and theoretically has no access to the newspapers.

Other illustrations of possible contempts include:

1. Grossly careless or overdramatic handling of courtroom news.
2. Caustic cartoons depicting the trial.
3. Publishing or broadcasting stories about juvenile delinquents when forbidden by law, order, or rule of court.
4. Stories which interfere with the investigations of a grand jury.
5. Photographs taken in court against court rules or orders.

Even in the absence of a written rule, a judge has power to punish as a contempt any photographic expedition into his courtroom. As photographers who have been fined or imprisoned well know, the punishment is imposed by the very judge who believes that the dignity of his forum has been violated.

Writer's Refusal to Testify

Now and then the refusal of a reporter or editorial writer to reveal confidential sources of information results in punishment for contempt. The general rule is: Neither the guarantees of the First Amendment in respect to a free press nor any rule of privilege gives the reporter or editor, as a witness in a libel suit, a right to refuse to disclose the sources of the information on which the challenged writing is based. In a few states there are ameliorating statutes.

JUSTICE UNDISTURBED

Judicial decisions say that "the first requisite of a court of justice is that its machinery be left undisturbed." Hence, anyone who intrudes himself into the due and orderly administration of justice is guilty of contempt of court and subject to punishment.

Assume, for instance, a suit based upon permanent and deforming injuries to a five-year-old girl. The little girl has not been exhibited to the jury; she has not even been taken into the courtroom. A newspaper or newscaster describes her as a "bright and happy little girl" playing in the hall of the courthouse, "not at all depressed by her misfortune." In the courtroom the parents and their attorney are presenting their case under the theory that since the accident the little girl has been depressed and unable to join with her friends gaily in play as she did before the accident. *Query:* Would the news story constitute a comment on the evidence so as to interfere with the administration of justice?

WHEN THE CASE IS OVER

Most courts hold that comment on concluded cases cannot be punished as contempt—there might be a libel of the judge, though no contempt of the tribunal. However, occasional deviations say that a violent statement touching a concluded case may be a contempt. The rationale is that such a statement degrades the court and tends to destroy public confidence and impair the court's efficiency in subsequent litigation. Courts differ as to whether a case already tried and now on appeal, or one where the time within which to appeal has not yet run, is still pending or is over so far as contempt of court is concerned.

Truth Not a Defense

The truth of a story is not a defense against a citation for contempt. Perhaps the truth hurts most. Punishment may be by fine, or imprisonment, or both.

Possible contempts are not everyday problems, as are incipient libels and violations of the right of privacy. Neither writers nor administrative personnel can be expected to develop an adequate discretion in respect to contempts—not even the courthouse reporter can do this. As an officer of the court, your attorney will sense the situation.

CHAPTER 12

PICTURES—STILL
AND MOVING

A room hung with pictures is a room hung with thoughts.

SIR JOSHUA REYNOLDS

As already shown, contempts of court may stem from the taking of pictures. Violations of the right of privacy are as often predicated on the picture as on the story. Hence, photographers are invited to consider the preceding and next succeeding chapters as well as this to be their special domain.

I. LIBEL

The fundamentals of libel apply to photographs and their captions. The privileges are essentially the same.

LIBELOUS PICTURES

Error in identification is probably the most frequent source of libel based on pictures. Usually that is a "someone-blundered" situation. Perhaps years ago the picture was mislabeled in the morgue. Perhaps the writer of captions or cut lines made a mistake—excusable or otherwise. Not all libel based on pictures can be debited against photographers. But much of it can be, and most of that can be traced to careless identification. In contrast to script, which may be false, an accurately identified picture is in itself true.

ILLUSTRATIONS

Typical situations resulting in suits for libel include the following:

1. Picture of two or more persons at the jailhouse, the wrong one being identified as the character being booked.

2. Picture of "men n.entioned" in the "blackmail scandal," plaintiff not being singled out as an innocent bystander until near the end of the story.

3. Picture of a movie starlet in a scandal; wrong starlet or scandal.

4. Picture of one or a few out of many persons held by the police for questioning, captions giving the impression that some of those pictured are suspects, not merely potential witnesses.

5. Picture of the scene of an auto accident involving a crime, such as drunken driving, without making plain who are the accused and who are the injured innocent or mere bystanders.

6. Picture of a solid citizen erroneously identified as doing something amounting to any libel per se described in Chapter 3.

7. Feature story about customs inspectors, telling of their uncanny knowledge of hiding places, plus a picture of identifiable persons passing through a customs inspection, thus suggesting that they are customs suspects.

Plaintiff had testified before a congressional committee as to how he had refused to take part in an alleged fraud. The *Boston Traveller* ran his picture with those of two other men under a banner headline: "SETTLEMENT UPPED $2000—$400 KICKBACK TOLD." No reference was made to plaintiff in the accompanying article. The court was unable to decide that as a matter of law there was *not* a libel per se. So the question was one for determination by the jury.

Among other principal sources of libel from photographs may be listed:

1. Violations of conditions imposed by subject.
2. Retouching a picture to accentuate seminudity, however flattering the result may be.
3. Deleting part of the picture; superimposed or fake pictures; distortions and optical illusions.
4. Any picture accompanying defamatory text or cut lines.

When a picture is taken despite the objections of the subject, or when the photographer has shouldered his way into a private home or other unauthorized spot to take it, the defense of the picture is made doubly difficult.

CARTOONS AND SKETCHES

Sketches of current events are subject to the same tests as photographs. Cartoons are usually in the category of comment and criticism. They are subject to the rules of Chapter 8. Comic strips are mostly concerned with clearly fictitious characters. A few have created libel problems because of the use of the name of an individual.

MOTION PICTURES

Newsreels are subject to the fundamental rules and gauges applicable to other media reporting current events. A play will be judged as would a published story. If it is based on someone's life, a violation of the right of privacy may enter.

TELEVISION

The principles touching libel which apply to still photographs and text carry over to their ultimate—the broadcasting of pictures in motion plus accompanying sound. The picture broadcast must be judged in conjunction with what is said over television, much as the picture on paper must be interpreted in relation to the printed text.

II. COURTROOM PHOTOGRAPHY

The taking of pictures (still, moving, or televised) during the course of a trial contrary to the rules or specific instructions of the court would likely lead to contempt proceedings against the photographer and his employer. To that extent, this is a proper subject for the preceding chapter.

News photography and television with the permission of the trial judge would not be a contempt. The question would be: Was there a fair trial? As to that aspect, the following discussion is a natural part of Chapter 16—"Free Speech—Fair Trial." But that chapter is concerned with all media.

Since this chapter specializes in photography, we bring the courtroom here.

RULES OF COURT

Believing that the taking of pictures in court is not fitting and results in improper publicizing of judicial proceedings, most states—by rule of court or otherwise—have mandates to the effect that:

> The taking of photographs in the courtroom, during sessions of the court or recesses between sessions, and the broadcasting or televising of court proceedings detract from the essential dignity of the proceedings and distract the witness in giving his testimony.

The precise wordings differ somewhat. Usually the rule does not apply to a ceremonial such as a naturalization proceeding.

The federal rules of criminal procedure are to the effect that the taking of photographs in the courtroom during the progress of judicial proceedings or radio broadcasts from the courtroom shall not be permitted. This federal prohibition is commonly observed in civil trials.

The Trend—More or Less Photography?

Before June 7, 1965, many newsmen who believed photography to be a desirable medium for reporting trials optimistically forecast that refinements in technology would bring a relaxing of judicial opinion to the effect that courtrooms must be forbidden ground for photography. Then came the Billie Sol Estes decision by the United States Supreme Court. It has three principal aspects: (i) its immediate impact upon televising criminal trials, (ii) other courtroom photography in criminal cases, and (iii) its probable long-range effect upon photographing or televising.

Televising Criminal Trials

Splitting five to four, the court upset the conviction of Estes because the trial was televised. The majority of the court declared that "televising of criminal trials denies to defendants their constitutional right of due process of law"—a fair trial. The opinion asserts that "experience teaches that there are numerous situations in which it might cause actual unfairness—some so subtle as to defy detection by the accused or control by the judge." Four possibilities were described in considerable detail; we can but list them:

1. Potential impact upon the jurors—deemed of the greatest significance.
2. The quality of testimony will often be impaired.

3. Additional responsibility the presence of television places on the judge. He must supervise an unnecessary distraction. He should not be put to the initial decision of whether or not to permit it, particularly in states where judges are selected at the ballot box.
4. It is a form of mental—if not physical—harassment of defendant, resembling a police line-up or third degree.

The Chief Justice begins his concurring opinion by agreeing that "the televising of criminal trials is inherently a denial of due process." He based his conclusion on three grounds:

1. The televising of trials diverts the trial from its proper purpose in that it has an inevitable impact on all the trial participants.
2. It gives the public the wrong impression about the purpose of trials, thereby detracting from the dignity of court proceedings and lessening the reliability of trials.
3. It singles out certain defendants and subjects them to trials under prejudicial conditions not experienced by others.

Four justices thought otherwise. "It is important," they said, "to remember that we move in an area touching the realm of free communication," and should "be wary of imposing any per se rule which, in the light of future technology, might serve to stifle or abridge true First Amendment rights."

In his concurring opinion Mr. Justice John M. Harlan wrote: "The Estes trial was a heavily publicized and highly sensational affair. I therefore put aside all other types of cases." It may be inferred that in a case involving less notoriety he might have decided differently. If so, only four justices voted to hold televised criminal trials to be constitutionally infirm, whatever the circumstances. But it is not likely that a trial judge will permit television in a criminal proceeding on the chance that the Supreme Court might decide that in his particular case there was no prejudice to the accused.

OTHER COURTROOM PHOTOGRAPHY IN CRIMINAL CASES

The Estes decision is built around television—an appendix includes seven full-page pictures of television gear. It should not be construed as erecting a constitutional ban against all photography, even in criminal cases.

However, as indicated, the Canons of Judicial Ethics bar the taking of photographs in the courtroom during sessions of the court or between sessions. Many rules of court are to the same effect.

Courtroom photography other than television has not yet been banned as *always* resulting in an unfair trial. If a particular judge clearly permits it, punishment will not descend upon the head of the photographer. But that judge may find his conduct challenged and in due course criticized by an appellate tribunal.

PROBABLE LONG-RANGE EFFECT UPON CIVIL SUITS

About the same may be said in respect to the trend in civil cases. An occasional judge will permit courtroom photography if all parties to the litigation agree and no witness objects.

The current formerly believed running in favor of courtroom photography has been reversed. Where it will stabilize, no one can foretell.

The Estes decision should be remembered as an example of the *kind of conduct* which invites restrictive court decisions and legislative bans. This comment applies to libel and right of privacy as much as to photography. Had the invasion of the courtroom and its environs by television been less flamboyant, perhaps the scales would have tipped the other way. The weight of one judge would have sufficed.

Except for this excursion into the courtroom, libel and contempts have been the topics. Though a person libeled may be entitled to receive compensation for emotional distress resulting from the defamation, libel is primarily concerned with the individual's reputation in the minds of other people. Its main tests are external.

Right of privacy protects the individual's interest in freedom from emotional distress. Its tests are subjective, internal. We turn now to this kindred subject.

CHAPTER 13

RIGHT OF PRIVACY

A newspaper should not invade private rights or feeling without sure warrant of public right as distinguished from public curiosity.

Canons of Journalism of the American Society of Newspaper Editors

THE right of privacy—the right to be let alone—as increasingly enforced in the courts is a relatively new facet of the law. In 1890 Louis D. Brandeis and his law partner wrote an article, "The Right to Privacy." Denouncing the flamboyant journalism of that day, they contended that invasions upon privacy were subjecting individuals "to mental pain and distress, far greater than could be inflicted by mere bodily injury." They asserted that the press was "overstepping in every direction the obvious bounds of propriety and of decency." They discerned a common law right, "forged in the slow fires of the centuries," entitling a person to redress if his privacy was wrongly invaded.

Here and there judges began to follow their reasoning; a few legislatures took statutory notice of the problem. Though other courts and legislatures refused, today the right to be let alone, to be unmolested in private affairs, is recognized as legally enforcible. The Restatement of Torts says: "A person who unreasonably and seriously interferes with another's interest in not having his affairs known to others *or his likeness exhibited to the public,* is liable to the other" (italics added).

Perhaps the trend of the times is indicated by an assertion in the Universal Declaration of Human Rights: "No one shall be subjected to arbitrary interference with his privacy, family, home or correspondence, nor to attacks upon his honor and reputation. Everyone has the right to the protection of the law against such interference or attacks." There the new right against interference with privacy is named before the ancient right of redress for libel.

THE NEWS MAY BE PUBLISHED

However, the situation must not be overstated. Certainly this right of privacy does not prohibit publication and broadcasting of matters of public interest. The news may be made known and newsworthy pictures printed and broadcast even though the subject came unwillingly into the limelight. Following the language of the Supreme Court of Kentucky: There are times when one, whether willingly or not, becomes an actor in an occurrence of public or general interest. When this takes place, he emerges from his seclusion. It is not an invasion of his right of privacy to publish his photograph with an account of the occurrence.

Many persons are in themselves newsworthy. When a person becomes a public character, he relinquishes his right of privacy or at least great areas of privacy.

The general rules may be summarized by saying that the right of privacy does not exist where:

1. The subject has himself published or broadcast the matter or given consent—but consent or waiver can be rescinded before the broadcast or publication.

2. The subject is in the news because of his prominence or activities.
3. He is an object of legitimate public interest because of some event. (But some judges are beginning to speak of an area of privacy which may not be invaded with impunity even though related to the newsworthy event; for instance, in the case of a gruesome picture.)
4. Under the law of libel there would be a privileged communication.
5. The subject is a corporation or public institution. *Caveat:* A strictly family type corporation might be an exception to this exception.

The prohibition is merely against the publicizing of private affairs with which the public has no legitimate concern or the wrongful intrusion (the bad taste, if you please, of an intrusion) into private activities in such a manner as to cause mental suffering, shame, or humiliation to a person of ordinary sensibilities.

Good Taste the Essence

Courts have said that the right protects against "the unwarranted appropriation or exploitation of one's personality." The meaning and scope of that vague phrase will be determined only if a considerable number of cases reach courts of final jurisdiction. The theme of this chapter is: *If publishers and broadcasters will exercise a modicum of discretion and use the good taste which, as individuals, they exercise in their own affairs, the now evolving right of privacy will not become a greater menace.* If it is given food on which to grow, this newborn right could become a Frankenstein which might deter either publication or broadcasting of material which should be known to the public and which gives news much of its human interest.

Stale News

May a person, once in the news, by lapse of time reacquire a right of privacy as to his past life? A child prodigy, a failure as an adult, sued the *New Yorker* because of an unvarnished factual account of his life. The court denied recovery; there was a certain continuing public interest in what he had turned out to be.

An ex-convict sued the National Broadcasting Company because it televised a dramatized fictional version of his conviction for murder and later pardon. He was not identified. There was no actionable invasion of privacy. But a former prostitute who had metamorphosed into a respectable matron was successful in a suit against the publishers of the unsavory incidents of her past. The California court found a constitutional right to "pursuing and obtaining safety and happiness."

Contrary to plaintiff's request, the *Los Angeles Examiner* published a story concerning the third marriage of a former city attorney and political figure. It told of "hectic times" during his career, including unpleasant details. The court held that this did not constitute a violation of his right of privacy.

Sundry Pictures

Courts have given consideration to a theory denominated a "relational right of privacy." This means, for instance, the right of parents to be spared suffering from the publishing or broadcasting of pictures of a son (not himself newsworthy) killed under grotesque or disgraceful circumstances. A story of a deformed, stillborn baby, plus a picture taken without the consent of the parents, ended in a judgment against the publisher.

Held to create a right of action were:

1. The picture of a husband and wife in an affectionate position as part of an article on "Love"—held not warranted by public need or the public character of the twain.

2. A photograph of a child as she lay in the street after an auto accident as part of a later safety-first article entitled, "They Asked to Be Killed." Original publication of the picture as news was not a violation.

3. A photograph of a female taxi driver as an illustration in a libelous article directed against taxi drivers in general. Plaintiff was not mentioned by name or otherwise identified.

4. Too vivid cheesecake (photograph or television) in relation to the sensibilities, vocation, and environment of the subject.

Three months after the event, a magazine ran a story concerning the killer of plaintiff's husband, a policeman slain in line of duty. It was entitled, "If You Love Me, Slip Me a Gun." The publisher claimed the article was a factual account of the escape of a dangerous criminal, the heroism of law enforcement officers, and the eventual triumph of justice. The court disagreed, saying that the story "makes a strong appeal to the idle and prurient." The widow's picture was used. She had a good cause of action against the magazine.

In another action against the same publisher it was held that the widow and children of a man who had been kicked to death by a gang of adolescents could not recover for invasion of their privacy by an accurate factual account, illustrated with their pictures, three months after the homicide.

The two decisions are not in conflict. The "Slip Me a Gun" story was sensationalized. It was not news. The story of the juvenile delinquents was accurate; the court thought it still had news value.

PUBLIC EVENTS

A person attending a public event may be televised, or his picture may be taken as part of the audience. Someone who is traveling or is in a public place cannot object to being pictured as part of a general scene. For instance, a television camera "panning" the audience might televise a recognizable individual. But, without his consent (unless he himself is newsworthy), he should not be featured in a close-up shot.

Discussing "the area of privacy which may not be invaded even in this modern era of television," the Court of Appeals of New York said:

> One traveling upon the public highway may expect to be televised, but only as an incidental part of the general scene. So, one attending a public event such as a professional football game may expect to be televised in the status in which he attends. If a mere spectator, he may be taken as part of the general audience, but may not be picked out of a crowd alone, thrust upon the screen and unduly featured for public view. . . .

If, however, an individual is a public personage, or an actual participant in the public event, or if some newsworthy incident affecting him is taking place, his picture may be played up to its full news value.

ILLUSTRATIONS
1. An innocent actor in a great tragedy, whether limited, as a murder in his family, or widespread, such as flood, fire, or earthquake.
2. A deliberate exhibitionist, such as a provable and public attempt at suicide—window ledge, for instance.

It is hoped that the apogee has been reached when an attorney representing a marine returning from the wars felt justified in bringing suit because a paper published a picture of him taken at the dock while he was weeping on his mother's shoulder. The theory was that the picture was an invasion of his privacy and humiliating to a hardy marine.

COMMERCIAL USE

When advertising is involved, the rule is more strict. In some states, there may be a misdemeanor.

A violation may stem from the unauthorized use of a name or picture in advertising without an otherwise objectionable connotation. All of the following were so held:

1. Plaintiff was photographed in a store. Without her consent, her photograph was published to advertise the business.
2. Without her consent, a picture of the plaintiff—doubtless beautiful—was used in a cosmetic advertisement.
3. Displaying plaintiff's picture in an ad and stating he was a policyholder with defendant life insurance company.
4. "Before" and "after" pictures of plaintiff in trunks purporting to show his development before and after taking a physical improvement course. Ten years before he had proudly given consent to the use of the pictures. The second run, without a renewal of the permission, was an invasion of his right of privacy.
5. The War Department released a photograph showing Reed as a member of a team of optical experts engaged in repairing lenses at the front. Reed had no right of privacy against the army's use of his picture in furtherance of its policy in building home-front morale. But this gave no license to an optical company to use the picture for advertising its wares. Reed's right to privacy was violated.

TRUTH NOT A DEFENSE

In sharp contrast to libel, truth is not a defense where right of privacy is concerned. Nor is absence of malice a complete defense. Plaintiff need not prove special damage. Hence, in that respect, a violation of the right of privacy is akin to a libel per se. Even punitive damages have been allowed.

RESURRECTING THE DEAD

As in the case of libel of a person deceased, there is no actionable invasion of the right of privacy by penetrating the affairs of the dead if the living members of the family are let alone.

ILLUSTRATIONS

1. The widow and Sonny Capone sued because of a telecast depicting the notorious career of the gangster. They were not pictured or referred to in any of the broadcasts. Sonny had been a boyhood friend of the president of Desilu Productions and had begged him to refrain from producing "The Untouchables."

One of the three judges of the Court of Appeals found defendant's conduct "reprehensible" and that the "profit motive outweighed any concern about injury to innocent people." Reluctantly, he agreed that the widow and son did not have a cause of action for invasion of right of privacy.

2. The *Saturday Evening Post* used the title "Highway Robbery" with an article telling of bribery and dishonest construction practices during the building of federal-aid highways in New Mexico. Plaintiffs' deceased father had been the contractor. They claimed invasion of their right of privacy. They were not mentioned in the article.

The United States Court of Appeals recognized "a right to seclusion, [and] to freedom from public disclosure of personal matters of private life." But analogizing to defamations, the decision was that the action does not survive the death of the party whose privacy was invaded unless the complaining party's privacy was also invaded.

States Differ

It would be easy to arrange a neat tabulation purporting to list states that clearly recognize the right of privacy. Some states still deny it. As to others, it is impossible to make a sharp classification. Moreover, even in states that do recognize the rule, the cases are so limited in number that more definite guideposts cannot be set up.

In the few states that still deny the right, it is equally important to avoid a violation. The first publisher or broadcaster who transgresses the rule recognized in other states may bring it into his own state, to the detriment of every publisher and broadcaster.

CHAPTER 14

RADIO AND TELEVISION

> *Zeal is very blind, or badly regulated,*
> *when it encroaches upon the rights of*
> *others.*
>
> QUENSEL

THE fundamentals of libel and of the right of privacy apply to communication by radio and television. In addition, broadcasters have unique problems. Some are inherent in their method of communication—broadcasts in contrast to the printed page. Others are created by fiat of regulatory bodies. The latter, particularly those resulting from the impact of the Communications Act of 1934 as amended and administered by the Federal Communications Commission in respect to political broadcasts, are reserved for the next chapter.

I. IN GENERAL

Though a newspaper's deadline may leave little time for deliberation, the editorial rooms do have an opportunity to read every word and scrutinize each picture before copy goes to press. In contrast, a broadcaster can never be completely sure that the script will be followed with fidelity, or that the television actor or speaker, by gesture or grimace, will not convey or emphasize a meaning not apparent in the words alone. Inflection of speech and gesture may carry as much or even more conviction than print or still picture.

In the absence of statutory relief, a station might be held liable for whatever it puts on the air, even though the utterance was a departure from script in defiance of instructions that forbid ad-libbing and in spite of seemingly adequate precautions taken by broadcaster's personnel.

DUE CARE

By common law reasoning some courts protected a station not at fault; but others did not. About forty legislatures have met the problem by enacting laws to the effect that a broadcaster shall not be liable unless it is alleged and proved that he (meaning the station's staff) has failed to exercise due care to prevent the publication or utterance.

Whether the station exercised due care may become a question of fact to be decided by a jury. Failure to observe a libel per se in a manuscript submitted by a speaker or in a script prepared by the staff would almost certainly show lack of due care, whether the error stemmed from carelessness or ignorance. A station that permitted a person ignorant of the laws of libel to pass on copy would not be exercising due care. In short, the statutes do not relieve broadcast personnel from requirements of alertness comparable to those for journalists who communicate on paper.

There is not yet a body of case law from which can be gleaned rules clearly delineating due care. A speaker departs from his approved script—how many libelous words may he say before there is a failure in due care if he is not cut off? Or he makes small departures, each almost a libel or violation of privacy but not quite. Then, in one clause, before he can be cut off, he says something clearly actionable. Were small departures harbingers of the actionable statement so that in exercise of due care the station should have substituted a Strauss waltz?

As to writers of radio and television scripts, producers, directors, continuity editors, announcers, and all other station personnel, the proper caution is:

> Statutes ameliorating common law rules will help only if the broadcaster has been as careful as he can. The statutes will help defend if and only if due care has been exercised. So, as a practical matter, station personnel should be as informed, alert, and careful in states with protective statutes as in states without them.

NETWORK PROGRAMS

Some statutes protect a station broadcasting a network program if it is not the station of origin. How such statutes will be construed in aggravated situations where due care would have prevented the tort is not yet known.

WHAT LAW APPLIES

State boundaries are no barrier to a broadcast. A court may hold that the final act of the broadcast occurred in a receiving set a thousand miles away, rather than in the studio. If a person resident and known in that distant state is defamed or his right of privacy violated, the law of that state may govern in the suit against the station. For this additional reason, therefore, except as to discretionary decisions by management, a protective statute should be thought of as a defense, not as justification for laxity.

II. CONTROVERSIAL ISSUES AND FAIR PLAY

No legally qualified candidate is on the air during this chapter.

A newspaper, magazine, or book may be dedicated to the advancement of a point of view. Its field may be economic, religious, social change, partisan politics—or any its sponsor chooses. It can be biased and present but one approach.

Not so with broadcasting. Following the language of the Communications Act, the station has an obligation "to operate in the public interest and to afford reasonable opportunity for the discussion of conflicting views on issues of public importance." A station need not make its facilities available for controversial discussion of—say—the proposed freeway. But if it does, reasonable opportunity must be granted for the presentation of contrasting viewpoints.

CONTROVERSIAL ISSUES

The rule is that when station time is granted for radio or television broadcasts concerning a controversial subject of public nature—any subject where opinions differ—the people on both sides of the question have a right to be heard. It matters not whether the program is commercial or sustained. Federal Communications Commission policy requires that a balanced presentation be afforded both sides. Whenever possible, the station should seek out the other side and offer time. Certainly, if equivalent time is requested, it should be made available if it is possible to do so.

FAIR PLAY

Such are the requirements of fair play—the "fairness doctrine" —in the public interest. What constitutes fair play in a specific situation? That is the question. It cannot always be answered precisely, as in the case of statutory equal opportunity between legally qualified candidates—though even there, as will be seen, managerial discretion comes into play.

Some legal games have definite rules, easy to announce: Drive on the right side; a conveyance of real estate must be signed before a notary. Others are vague. "Reasonable." Just what does it mean when one must act "reasonably"?

The fairness doctrine cannot be reduced to a stencil. Once a controversial issue is put on the air, management must, in good faith, allocate time so that principal viewpoints can be brought to public attention. The good faith is exercised in the framework of inherent importance, public interest, pressure for air time because of other affairs which must be made known (war, earthquakes, politics, matters of great local interest, and so on), operational problems of the station, and all other factors which properly influence allocations of time. Perhaps it can be boiled down by saying: "Be intellectually honest, unswayed by personal preferences."

Fair Playing with Libel

Unless a qualified political candidate is on the air discussing the controversial issue, the usual rules of libel apply, as modified by the statutes just described, which are designed to ameliorate the extra-hazardous situation of the broadcaster. The station may also be held for violations of the right of privacy or contempt of court.

Replies to Attacks

In Chapter 9 we touched upon reply to an attack as a defense to a libel action. It is the duty of a station to offer to those who are attacked an opportunity to answer the charges which have been hurled against them. But (except as to legally qualifed candidates) the Communications Act does not grant the station exoneration from liability for libel incident to the reply.

Subject to available defenses, the station is responsible for the defamation present in the first attack. The station will be responsible also for libel in an offensive counter-offense, subject to the defenses discussed in previous chapters—with special emphasis on the duty of the station to furnish a forum for the reply. Script should have been read and corrected before the first libelous attack. The answer must be read and made safe, with the right of reply in mind.

CHAPTER 15

POLITICAL BROADCASTS

*In politics, merit is rewarded by the pos-
sessor being raised, like a target, to a
position to be fired at.*

BOVEE

A STATION is not required to permit the use of its facilities by any
political candidate—more precisely, by the first to whom broadcast time is made available. But if the station grants time to one
candidate, it must allow time to all who are running for that
office.

The mandates applicable to broadcasts by qualified candidates differ in kind from the rules that apply to their advocates
and all others.

I. BROADCASTS BY CANDIDATES

The Communications Act states that if a station permits any
person who is a legally qualified candidate for any public office
to use its facilities, equal opportunity must be afforded all other
such candidates for that office, with no power of censorship
over the material broadcast.

The requirements of the act as implemented by the Federal

Communications Commission are such that a sharp distinction must be drawn between broadcasts by (i) a "legally qualified candidate" and (ii) anyone else. As to the former, the station may face delicate dilemmas in respect to possible libel. In extreme situations it may have to choose the lesser of two evils. Shall the first candidate be refused time on the station because of the risk that some of his utterances will be libelous or obscene, plus the risk—almost certainty—that rival candidates will demand an equal opportunity and perhaps retort in kind? Or should the station refuse all candidates for that office and endure the abuse that will follow each refusal?

Legally Qualified Candidates

If a station blandly assumes that every seeker of publicity who announces himself for office is within the statute, it may have to prove the truth of a scurrilous broadcast or pay damages to those defamed. Hence it is important to be able to distinguish between "legally qualified candidates" and those who are not.

Passing, for the moment, candidates for the presidency (or vice-presidency) of the United States, the status of a candidate must be decided in accordance with state and local law applicable to that election. In briefest form: A candidate is legally qualified if it appears that he will be on the ballot or will be put there by sticker or by writing in and be voted on in the coming election and, if elected, is eligible to serve.

When the candidate's name is not to be on the printed ballot, the station should not give him laissez faire as a qualified candidate unless it is clear he is making a serious race for the office. A candidate requesting statutory privileges carries the burden of proving that he is a legally qualified candidate. The station may make proper requirements in respect to proving qualifications.

Presidental Candidates

The nominee of the national convention of a recognized party is a candidate for President—or vice-president—of the United States. State and local requirements as to candidacies do not control—as they would in a mayoralty or gubernatorial election.

Communists

Because of the provisions of the Communist Control Act, a candidate of the Communist party is not entitled to equal time. This rule may be changed.

> #### Caution
> Do not spread this exception to exclude a candidate of another party merely because he personally is or is thought to be a Communist.

Other Candidates for that Office

When a candidate demands time equal to that of the candidate who has been on the air, the station may require him to prove that he and his opponent are both "legally qualified candidates" for the same office or are rivals for nomination in the same primary.

Prior to convention or primary, the two or more parties are considered separately. Jones and Baldwin are both candidates for the Republican nomination, by primary or convention. If Jones is on the air, Baldwin is entitled to equal opportunity.

But Carrie, a candidate for nomination by one of the other parties, is not entitled to equal time; his is a separate race. Nor does time afforded a winning candidate in the primary of itself entitle his opponents in the final election to equal opportunity.

Use of Broadcasting Station

If a candidate is permitted "to use a broadcasting station," all other candidates for the same office shall be afforded an equal opportunity. A 1959 amendment to the act helps define the meaning of "use." It provides that appearance on any

- (i) bona fide newscast or (ii) news interview;
- (iii) bona fide news documentary—if the appearance of the candidate is merely incidental to the presentation of the subject of the broadcast;
- (iv) on-the-spot coverage of bona fide news events—including political conventions and activities incidental thereto,

shall *not* be deemed to be "use." These helpful exceptions do not relieve management of the burden of exercising sound discretion in respect to the very broadcasts just listed.

The FCC held that to qualify under this provision: (i) the program must be a regularly scheduled program of the station or network in question, (ii) the determination of the content and format is made by the station or network and not the candidate, and (iii) the coverage was made by the station or network in the exercise of its news judgment and not for the candidate's political advantage.

Suppose a friendly newscaster questions the candidate at unusual length or the candidate becomes virtually unstoppable and pre-empts a disproportionate amount of time—has there been a "bona fide news interview"? If not, competitors must be afforded an equal opportunity. Or suppose the coverage of a news event results in one candidate being on the screen or his utterances on the air three times as much as his competitor? Five times? Ten times? At some point the bona fides of the newscast taper away and the lucky candidate is using the station instead of the station using him as an item of spot news.

Any use of the station not clearly within the listed exceptions should be considered a use, entitling the opponent to equal opportunity. Nor do the exceptions relieve a station of its obligation to operate in the public interest and to afford reasonable opportunity for the discussion of conflicting views on issues of public importance on the very broadcasts excepted from the equal opportunity mandate.

Who May Sue?

It has *not* been said that failure to afford equal time establishes a right of action on behalf of the disfavored candidate. Indeed, the opposite was held by the United States Court of Appeals in an action for damages ($25,000,000) brought by a disgruntled candidate for mayor of Chicago. The basic purpose of the act is regulation in the public interest and not the creation of private rights. Enforcement is by the Federal Communications Commission. It considers the broadcasting of political programs as a criterion to be evaluated both in license renewal proceedings and in contests for radio or television construction permits. And the reputation of the station may be affected adversely by plausible charges that it is giving a favored candidate extra time over the public's air.

No Censorship of Candidates

The station may not censor—may not edit—the script of a legally qualified candidate. The station may not delete libel. The balancing factor is that the station is not legally responsible for defamatory or other improper statements (e.g., obscenities) by the candidate. A leading decision points out that if a station were not protected against suit the situation would be untenable, because "unless a station refuses to permit any candidate to talk at all, the [law] would sanction the unconscionable result of permitting civil and perhaps criminal liability to be imposed for the very conduct the statute demands of the station," and any rule to the contrary would be "in conflict with traditional concepts of fairness."

SECURE ADVANCE COPY; REASON TOGETHER

If the request is made of all candidates for the office in question, the station may require script in advance of the broadcast. If there is any doubt as to the good taste or emotional stability of the candidate, this may be a wise thing to do. The rule against censorship connotes denial of any examination of thought or expression designed to prevent (forbid) publication of objectionable material. Nevertheless, if it is made plain that there will be no censorship or forced deletions, management may reason quietly with the candidate and suggest that because of possible libel or other ill, he may wish to change the text. Perhaps he will quickly agree that it is good politics to do so. The conversation must be a soft sell. A promptly dictated log for the files is desirable; the candidate might later claim censorship.

OBSCENE STATEMENTS

Few candidates will intentionally include obscenity—it would alienate voters; nearly every candidate will follow a friendly suggestion to delete material which is in palpable bad taste. If he does not, and his opponent has used the station, he must be given equal time.

FORECAST
Someday, over a nationwide hookup, an eccentric candidate will shock the public with vulgarities not related to campaign issues. Then the law will be amended to permit the station to delete that kind of trash.

EQUAL OPPORTUNITIES

The station must "afford equal opportunities to all other" qualified candidates, not merely to the principal opponent of the one first on the air.

The equal opportunity need not be measured with scientific precision. The day of the week and hour need not be the same —indeed, an opportunity to the second or third or fourth candidate to reply quickly may be the essence of equality. Management must, in good faith, do its best to afford each candidate equally desirable time—as much of it to one as to another.

PRIMARY AND FINAL CAMPAIGNS

Though it is permissible to treat the primary and final election campaigns separately from the standpoint of equal opportunity, a broadcaster's obligations in respect to controversial issues might make it unwise to allow a drastic imbalance to occur. For instance: Suppose that during the primary campaign candidate Webster is permitted to purchase or is given ten hours of time, whereas candidate Green requests only two hours. It might be difficult to refuse a timely request by Green for more time in the runoff than is requested by Webster so that in the aggregate Green may have as much time as Webster had. Then of course Webster might counter by demanding equal time measured by the final election alone. If the station makes a genuine effort to be fair the dilemmas will probably dissolve —or be forgotten after election day.

NO CHANCE TO BE NOMINATED

Not every crackpot who announces himself as a candidate is actually a legally qualified candidate within the meaning of the act prior to the time he is on the ballot.

Nevertheless, it must be stressed that an announced candidate cannot be refused equal opportunity merely because all political prognosticators say his chances are nil. Somewhere down the line a delicate but genuine distinction must be drawn between a zealot making a hopeless race and a maverick making noise. The zealot may make the ballot and someday his views be accepted as sound.

ILLUSTRATION

The mayor of a large city energetically sought the Democratic nomination for President in advance of the Democratic convention. Although he never had the backing of a significant number of the delegates, the FCC ruled that he was a qualified candidate. He convinced the FCC that he was making a bona fide race for the office by sending out brochures to all of the delegates from the various states, by having his name entered in one or two of the state Democratic primaries, and by rushing about and making speeeches attempting to line up votes.

II. By Advocates of Candidates and Others

We have been discussing rights which are personal to candidates only. The statutory requirement of "equal opportunity" does not reach requests for time by political parties, as such, campaign committees, and articulate supporters. Nor does candidate Jones have a legal right to demand an equal opportunity because Smith, not a candidate, has spoken over that station against Jones or in behalf of a rival candidate.

Other Campaign Speakers

When the candidate himself is not the speaker, the station may treat the broadcast as it would any other controversial program. Advance script should be required; language which appears to be defamatory or obscene or which tends to invade the right of privacy should be stricken. If the integrity or emotional stability of the speaker is doubtful, adequate safeguards that he will stay by his script may be imposed. In short, the station can do what is fair under the circumstances and in the public interest, without needlessly exposing itself.

The fairness doctrine, already discussed, comes into play. In the Times-Mirror Broadcasting controversy, the FCC ruled that where the broadcasting station had permitted a commentator or other persons not a candidate to take a partisan position on issues involved in a race for a political office and to attack one candidate or support another by direct or indirect identification, the station must immediately send a transcript of the pertinent continuity in each such program to the opposing candidates and should offer a comparable opportunity for an appropriate spokesman to answer the broadcasts.

Utterances by Public Officials

The statutory requirement of "equal opportunity" does not apply to a statement made by an official before he becomes a candidate, even though he may be planning to run. After he becomes a candidate, the situation is different. It often requires a fine discernment to determine when that Rubicon was crossed.

When a Candidate Is Libeled

When a candidate thinks he has been defamed, he may—probably will—demand an opportunity to respond. If the attack was by a duly qualified candidate, the answer has been given in Part I preceding.

If the libel was uttered by someone else, the handling of time for reply and the contents of the reply come under the principles applicable to fair play summarized in Part II of Chapter 14.

The reminder is: If a station permits a legally qualified candidate to respond to a person who is not so qualified (e.g., a supporter of an opposing candidate), the facilities of the station must be open to all other qualified candidates for that office. The caution is that if any third person first brings the black cloud of libel into view, it may be better to refuse the air to all candidates for that office.

OFF THE SCRIPT

As a practical matter, it is almost impossible to prevent a reckless speaker from ad-libbing libel. A number of states have enacted legislation designed to protect the station (not the speaker) when the station has used due care as to the script.

PRACTICAL PROTECTION

A station wants no libel broadcast over its facilities even though it will not have to pay damages because of what a candidate says. As a practical matter, how can management protect itself?

1. Remember that the die is cast when an affirmative answer is first given.
2. In acute situations where serious libel would be a rational prognosis, deny time to all the actual candidates for a particular office.
3. Put the spokesmen for candidates on the air only after review of script and adequate assurance that there will be no departure from it.
4. In the closing remarks on political ads (Chapter 5) the possibility of an indemnity agreement was suggested. As to advocates only (not a candidate) it may be useful here.

If after the broadcaster reasons with the candidate (without threat of censorship), there seems still to be danger but it is deemed advisable to permit the candidate to use the station:

1. Require him to submit by specified deadline either a full script or a complete outline of his talk.
2. Gently remind the candidate, his advertising agency, and, if possible, leading members of his campaign committee, that (though the station is exonerated) they may become involved in a suit based on libel or conspiracy, if their candidate defames his adversary. His committeemen may be grateful.

A Record of Requests

Records of all requests for political broadcast time should be kept as required by FCC regulations. It is prudent to make a tape of all political broadcasts. Otherwise the station may be put to the difficult task of proving what was actually said in rebuttal to the testimony of friends of the man who claims to have been libeled.

CHAPTER 16

FREE SPEECH—FAIR TRIAL

*For many years, lawyers and news media
have been battling each other with vehe-
mence and vigor.*

DEAN ERWIN N. GRISWOLD
Harvard Law School

THE current conflict in viewpoint in respect to news coverage of
trials—before, during, and in some instances after—is of major
significance. At one end of the spectrum are those who believe
the best interests of society are served by rules which afford
news media the utmost latitude. At the other end are those who
are convinced that present freedom in reporting trials must be
drastically curtailed.

The First (free speech) and the Sixth (fair trial) Amend-
ments to the federal Constitution are said to be on a collision
course. There are proposals to muzzle media. The most intense
clash of opinions originates in the field of crime, particularly
the coverage of pretrial news. Before attempting guidelines in
reporting events incident to arrest, accusation, and trial, we
must picture the opposing positions as best we can. This is not
an easy task. Bench and bar are not of one rigid conviction.
Policies of publishers differ sharply. The most that can be done

here is to report what is believed to be the consensus, then survey the best marked path.

Those who deal in news must remember that the courts have the final say. They may order and penalize. So first comes the consensus of bar and bench, the operational personnel of the law.

I. A Fair Trial

Conduct by personnel of news media that results in punishable contempt of court is discussed in Chapter 11. Here we are concerned with stories of trials which:

    (i) media management believes should be published in the public weal, or are at least permissible;

   (ii) judges and lawyers may believe make a fair trial impossible;

  (iii) under the circumstances, are not a contempt of court in the conventional sense—i.e., there may be a mistrial, but no serious contempt proceedings.

There may be a valid analogy between libel compared with right of privacy on one hand, and contempts compared with good taste in reporting news of trials on the other. Beyond the law of libel there is an increasing tendency on the part of the courts to protect the right of privacy, which means punishment of media for bad taste that injures someone. Beyond punishment for contempts as heretofore spelled out, there is a searching for formulas to prevent publication of matter deemed prejudicial to a fair trial—which again means bad taste in view of the potential trial of a man who is presumed to be innocent.

The Attorney General of the United States has issued a statement of policy applicable to personnel of the Department of Justice. It says that "certain types of information [news] generally tend to create dangers of prejudice." They are:

  (i) observations about a defendant's character;
 (ii) statements, admissions, confessions, or alibis attributable to a defendant;
(iii) references to investigative procedures, such as fingerprints, polygraph examinations, ballistic tests, or laboratory tests;
(iv) statements concerning the identity, credibility, or testimony of prospectve witnesses;
 (v) statements concerning evidence or arguments in the case, whether or not it is anticipated that such evidence or argument will be used at trial.

Personnel of the department may make public:

  (i) defendant's name, age, residence, employment, marital status, and similar background information;
 (ii) the substance or text of the charge, such as a complaint, indictment, or information;
(iii) the identity of the investigating and arresting agency and the length of the investigation;
(iv) the circumstances immediately surrounding an arrest, including the time and place of arrest, resistance, pursuit, possession and use of weapons, and description of items seized at the time of arrest.

Such is the viewpoint of the most important law office in the land. As a canon of conduct, it applies only to the Department of Justice. However, as a studied expression of legal opinion, its reach is broader. Certainly, in many situations, there will be a duty (and if not a duty, a right) to publish much more than lawyers and law enforcement officers see fit to release for publication. Nevertheless, the standards which members of the bench and bar set for themselves are important when determining the policy question of what should be published. In Part III of this chapter we will see promulgations where the varying viewpoints are reconciled and brought within one cover.

The New Jersey Supreme Court believes that unfair and pre-

judicial stories before and during trial of criminal cases are becoming more and more prevalent. The onus is spread upon
publishers, lawyers, and law enforcement officers. The court
interprets the Canons of Professional Ethics as banning certain
types of statements to news media by members of the bar—
alleged confessions; inculpatory admissions by the accused; that
the case is conclusive against the defendant; references to defendant's prior record of arrests or convictions and *also* statements respecting the innocence of the accused.

Writing in the *Trial Judge's Journal,* Mr. Justice John J.
Francis of that court calls upon trial judges to enforce the rules
of ethics. Trial judges countrywide were told that for some eight
months New York papers "had been filled"* with the accounts
of the murder of two young women. When a suspect confessed,
a police officer made the public announcement that "We
wouldn't have booked him if we weren't sure . . . we got the right
guy, no question about it." News media carried the quotation
and the circumstances surrounding the confession. The confession turned out to be untrue.

> It is hard to believe [the Justice said], . . . that if Whitmore
> [defendant] had gone to trial a jury could have been drawn
> which would not have included persons who had read or
> heard about his confession. Could such persons really
> remain uninfluenced by the damning pretrial publicity?
> Would any cautionary admonition by the judge, no matter
> how strong, really vitiate the effects of such publicity?
> Fortunately, Whitmore has not had to stand trial. It now
> appears that he is innocent, and that his confession was
> not true.

The eminent Justice concludes:

> Liberty of the press cannot be invoked in support of
> acts which invade the domain within which the authority

---

* *Query:* Does the use of the word "filled" meet the standard of
accuracy expected of newsmen when reporting crimes?

of the courts is exclusive. Legitimate interests of the press do not require that encroachments on the right to fair trial be sanctioned. If courts abdicate their responsibility in this area, not much can be asked of the news media.

Another issue of the *Trial Judge's Journal* lists eleven "current activities working toward a satisfactory solution of the problem." The problem and the searching for the solution will be in the foreground for many years to come.

II. FREE SPEECH

The Press-Bar Committee of the American Society of Newspaper Editors concludes that the claim of prejudice to fair trials by news coverage is "not proven"—is but a theory, not a fact. A plank of the committee is that a democratic community is not merely *entitled to know* promptly the facts about crime and the administration of justice, it *must know* them, else the very functioning of our government is endangered. Pointing to the need of intense and continuing public scrutiny, the committee said:

> A large part of the administration of justice in this country operates within, and is a part of, a political system: many judges, prosecutors and sheriffs are elected officials, subject to all the political pressures, good and bad, that characterize our democracy. If that part of the system is to operate successfully, another part, the press, must exercise without fetters both its responsibility for watching the administration of justice and its freedom to report what it observes.

Granting that it is too many if even a handful of defendants is denied a fair trial because of prejudicial publicity, the committee cited statistics indicating that instances of prejudicial result in relation to the bulk of criminal cases are trivial in number.

The committee had assessed "the feasibility of the principal restrictions that are common to most of the proposals made by concerned members of the bar and bench." The committee was convinced that "the repressions entailed by those proposals would not only cause a forfeiture of the public's credence in their news media but would withdraw the essential safeguard of public awareness and scrutiny from the processes of justice."

Stressing the need for continuous public scrutiny of the courts and the administration of justice, the committee was firm to the effect that if the press is to perform its functions, it "must not be bound by the same regulations that govern the operation of the law enforcement agencies and the courts." The committee was persuaded that "no set of specific rules can be written into a code of press conduct that will not do more harm than good."

This ASNE report concludes with an excellent statement of principles for consideration by the fourth estate. Media should:

   (i) rededicate themselves to the principle of reporting criminal affairs with restraint, good taste, and scrupulous regard for the rights of defendants, including the presumption of innocence, fair treatment, and fair trial by unprejudiced jurors;

  (ii) reaffirm their obligation to provide the public with full, objective, prompt, and honest information about criminal affairs, law enforcement, and the administration of justice;

 (iii) reject as impractical and harmful, attempts to restrict necessary news coverage by rigid regulations unduly limiting reporting of criminal and legal matters or suppressing information about them;

 (iv) undertake with open-mindedness and sincerity frequent discussions with the law enforcement agencies, the bar, and the bench, at all levels, for the purpose of creating mutual understanding of the problems involved, correcting abuses, resolving complaints, and furthering both full news coverage and fair trials.

Here and elsewhere we have given more lineage to "fair trial" than to "free speech." The latter is in the blood of all who gather and process news. The necessity of a fair trial as seen by judges and lawyers is less familiar ground. Both are essentials to a free society, though if forced to choose, Thomas Jefferson might have said that from the standpoint of preserving freedom for all citizens the few who unjustly are accused of crime must bear the risk of publicity that may be prejudicial (or perchance beneficial*) to his cause.

Starting with the premise that the opinion of the people is the basis of our government, Jefferson remarked: ". . . were it left to me to decide whether we should have a government without newspapers, or newspapers without a government, I should not hesitate a moment to prefer the latter." "But," he added, "I should mean that every man should receive those papers, and be capable of reading them." Had Jefferson been writing 175 years later, perforce he would have included the new media.

An analogy is found in privilege, absolute and qualified.

1. Public welfare requires that upon some occasions the innocent may be defamed maliciously and the lie repeated without redress to the injured.
2. Protection against crime and unjust imprisonments requires that steps leading to, as well as occurrences during and after a criminal proceeding, be subject to examination by the electors; this is another way of saying "be in the news," when the proceeding is considered newsworthy by someone other than officialdom.

Both 1 and 2 impose sacrifices upon an occasional innocent citizen who finds himself in the line of fire.

* In California, in a suit against a manufacturer of drugs, plaintiff argued that he was denied a fair trial because news media ignored the trial. Lack of publicity, his attorney pled, gave the jurors the impression that the case was of minor importance.

We now turn to more specific recommendations by study groups in respect to reporting crimes.

III. A Fair Balance

Divergent viewpoints and approaches have been summarized. Significant facets are these:

1. Media must admit many instances of flamboyant sensationalizing of trials—principally criminal, some civil. It is no wonder that judges and lawyers often feel a fair trial to be impossible.
2. Lawyers, defense and prosecution, and law enforcement officials must admit that all too often they feed the flame of excessive publicity and enjoy its light.
3. Consistent with the philosophy of the highest court in the land, the judges recognize that the courts must be open to public scrutiny—star chambers are not our way of life.
4. All groups want fair trials illuminated by free reporting so that the citizens will know that justice is evenhanded.

A committee comprised of representatives of the Massachusetts Newspaper Information Service, the Massachusetts Bar Association, and the Boston Bar Association, assisted by members of the Massachusetts judiciary, announced guidelines for news media and also for the bar.

For news media. To preserve the individual's rights to a fair trial, stories of crime should contain only a factual statement of the arrest and attending circumstances.

The following should be avoided:

1. Publication of interviews with subpoenaed witnesses after an indictment is returned.
2. Publication of the criminal record or discreditable acts of the accused after an indictment is returned or during the trial unless it is made part of the evidence in the court record. The defendant is being tried on the charge for which he is accused and not on his record.

3. Publication of confessions after an indictment is returned unless they are made a part of the evidence in the court record.

4. Publication of testimony stricken by the court unless reported as having been stricken.

5. Editorial comment, preceding or during trial, that tends to influence judge or jury.

6. Publication of names of juveniles involved in juvenile proceedings unless the names are released by the judge.

7. Publication of any "leaks," statements, or conclusions as to innocence or guilt, implied or expressed, by the police or prosecuting authorities or defense counsel.

For guidance of the bar. The Massachusetts committee continued with precepts for the guidance of the bar:

1. A factual statement of the arrest and circumstances and incidents thereof of a person charged with a crime is permissible, but the following should be avoided:

   a. Statements or conclusions as to the innocence or guilt, implied or expressed, by the prosecuting authorities or defense counsel.

   b. Out-of-court statements by prosecutors or defense attorneys to news media in advance of or during trial, stating what they expect to prove, whom they propose to call as witnesses, or public criticism of either judge or jury.

   c. Issuance by the prosecuting authorities, counsel for the defense, or any person having official connection with the case of any statements relative to the conduct of the accused, statements, "confessions," or admissions made by the accused or other matters bearing on the issue to be tried.

   d. Any other statement or press release to the news media in which the source of the statement remains undisclosed.

2. At the same time, in the interest of fair and accurate reporting, news media have a right to expect the cooperation of the authorities in facilitating adequate coverage of the law enforcement process.

The three teams—press, bar, and judiciary—have thus, informally, at least, agreed on fundamental rules for the Bay State. These are strict rules. Whether—without escape hatches to cope with special situations—they are too strict to be workable or generally acceptable, time will tell.

"In an effort to mitigate this conflict," the Oregon Association of Broadcasters collaborated with the Oregon Newspaper Publishers Association and the state bar in developing a statement of principles.

1. The news media have the right and the responsibility to print and to broadcast the truth.
2. However, the demands of accuracy and objectivity in news reporting should be balanced with the demands of fair play. The public has a right to be informed. The accused has the right to be judged in an atmosphere free from undue prejudice.
3. Good taste should prevail in the selection, printing, and broadcasting of the news. Morbid or sensational details of criminal behavior should not be exploited.
4. The decision concerning the publication of the news rests with the editor or news director. In the exercise of judgment he should consider that:
    (i) an accused person is presumed innocent until proved guilty;
    (ii) readers and listeners are potential jurors;
    (iii) no person's reputation should be injured needlessly.
5. The public is entitled to know how justice is being administered. However, it is unprofessional for a lawyer to exploit any medium of public information to enhance his side of a pending case. It follows that the public prosecutor should avoid taking unfair advantage of his position as an important source of news; this shall not be construed to limit his obligation to make available information to which the public is entitled.

These three Oregon associations concluded their report by testifying to "their continuing desire to achieve the best possible accommodation of the rights of the individual and the rights of the public when these two fundamental precepts appear to be in conflict with the administration of justice. . . ."

As in the case of related problems of publication (measuring libel; qualified privilege; possible violation of right of privacy), the answers to questions incident to reporting trials distill to common sense, good taste, and judgment applied (i) in the framework of the facts of a particular case, and (ii) with the fundamentals of free speech and fair trials in mind. "'Always" and "never" are words too strong for application here.

In recurrent situations, media cannot be expected to publish the meager account appropriate when a suspect is apprehended in a routine crime. Sometimes the importance of the accused or of the victim makes the crime a *cause célèbre*. Occasionally the very enormity of the crime—plus, perhaps, eyewitnesses, quick capture, and a confession—make a major story a must. In many a situation responsible media can scarcely suppress what is already known by word of mouth or from a publisher who plays up criminal news. There may be a duty to publish facts to counteract rampant rumor.

A decision that, in a particular instance, criteria applicable in most cases are inapplicable and that the crime should be reported with more than usual detail, should not be made lightly. Management should have in mind:

1. Possible libel—qualified privilege destroyed by excesses —see Chapter 7. (He may be found not guilty!)
2. Possible contempt of court—see Chapter 11.
3. Will the detailed story anger the judges and thus increase the pressures toward undesirable restrictions?
4. Is the story in the public interest?

The fundamental is—is the story unfair to either the accused, who is presumed innocent, or to the prosecution, which is charged with safeguarding society from the criminal element?

Confessions

Courts are holding that an accused has an absolute right to a full hearing on whether a confession he has signed was given voluntarily. If the judge rules it was a voluntary statement, it becomes admissible in evidence. If not truly voluntary, it will not be revealed to the jury.

Herein lies one of the knottiest problems. During the investigation period of a criminal case, media can (and sometimes do) withhold the news that the accused has signed a confession. If a juror has learned of the confession, he has learned it through other channels. (In a small town almost everyone might "know" of the confession except—apparently—media, which say nothing about it!)

Then comes the trial. In open court, but in the absence of the jury, the question of whether the confession was voluntary may be determined. If channels of communication are closed to jurymen, the fairness of the trial will not be affected. But if stories are published telling of the conflicting evidence in respect to the confession and these stories reach jurymen, obviously the defendant may be prejudiced, even though the confession itself is not admitted into evidence.

Whether media should ever agree not to publish what has been said in open court is a debatable question. In some places the hearing in respect to the validity of the confession is held prior to the trial itself, media withholding stories of that hearing. The results of this program are similar to those obtained when the hearing on the confession is delayed until the trial has begun, then the jurors are isolated so that they will have no knowledge of the stories published covering the evidence introduced while they were locked in the jury room.

It Could Happen Here

In England permissible news of criminal proceedings is strictly limited. In France freedom to report on judicial proceedings is threatened by a relatively new code of penal procedure. Police, magistrates, and lawyers may not reveal details of any criminal case; the public prosecutor or magistrate may make a written statement in order to negate "misleading news."

There are stirrings within some state legislatures. A maverick bill was introduced in a midwestern state which, if passed, would have imposed stringent criminal sanctions to prevent publication of anything except that the arrest has been made and, later, information admitted into evidence at the trial. It would not be a defense to the publisher that the news story had "no prejudicial effect on the trial," or that the story was true.

The best policy is to keep an even keel, avoiding the excesses which tempt retribution harmful to all, including the accused.

IV. Juvenile Courts

Philosophies and policies in respect to reporting proceedings in and ancillary to juvenile courts vary from alpha to omega. At one extreme are those who are convinced that there would be fewer youthful crimes if they were more generally reported and names given. Dramatic decreases in juvenile felonies are claimed for areas where juvenile hearings are open and participants usually identified in the news. Data favorable to open hearings are, however, challenged by investigators from social agencies.

At the other extreme are those who believe that to label a boy as a miscreant may mark him for life. The tendency will be to hurt rather than to deter. They say that some escapades are motivated by a desire for attention—publicity will encourage rather than discourage wrongdoing.

The nub of the divergence in viewpoints may, perhaps, be described another way. Those who favor publicity assert that the fine Oriental tradition of family responsibility will be furthered if the ignominy of one member of the family be visited on all. Families will see to it that their children behave if it is well known that the clan name will be shamed if they do not.

A SAMPLE OF OPINION

A survey was conducted by the *Wenatchee Daily World.*[*] Responses were from a fair sampling of law enforcement officers (70), newspaper editors (113), juveniles (601), and the general public (278)—all in the Pacific Northwest. Of all adults, 84.5 per cent believe that publicity helps reduce juvenile delinquency. Juveniles voted 49.5 per cent "yes" and 50.5 per cent "no."

Only 15 per cent of the adults said that publicity encourages juveniles to commit offenses; only 26.9 per cent of the juveniles agreed with them—73.1 per cent of the juveniles believe that publicity does *not* encourage crime.

Of the juveniles, 47.5 per cent favored publicizing even the first offense if grave and 98.3 per cent favored publicizing second offenders. The adult vote was 97 per cent in favor of exposing the second grave offense and 76.1 per cent for the first.

Sixty-five per cent of juveniles would publish the names of all traffic offenders; 83 per cent of the adults would do so.

There is a middle ground. Its tenets are stated in "Guides for Juvenile Court Judges in News Media Relations," promulgated by the National Council on Crimes and Delinquency. An ad-

---

[*] This paper won a certificate of merit in the American Bar Association's 1965 awards program "for outstanding published articles contributing to public understanding of the American system of law and justice."

visory council of judges from twenty-eight states sponsored the report. It recognizes that the juvenile court is an integral part of the judicial system. Therefore, the public has a right to know:

(i) the basic principles under which the court functions and the manner of its operations;
(ii) the kind of staff the court has;
(iii) the degree of the court's success or failure and the reason therefor;
(iv) the kinds of problems the court deals with day after day and the *impersonal* facts of cases which may illustrate these problems.

The report thus recognizes that the court has an obligation to make certain information accessible to news media—but it uses the word "impersonal."

Asserting that news media and judges should work together with confidence in, and respect for, each other, the council laid down guidelines to which, they believe, juvenile courts and news media can subscribe:

1. News media should be welcomed to all sessions of the juvenile court.
2. Responsibility for developing sound public interest in and understanding of the child, the community, and the court must be shared by the judge and the news media.
3. All official records should be open to the news media with the judge's consent, unless inspection is prohibited by statute.
4. Confidential reports should not be open to inspection by the press, except at the express order of the court.
5. The judge, *at his discretion,* may release the name or other identifying information of a juvenile offender in his court.
6. The court should strictly adhere to the Canons of Professional Ethics, which generally condemn the release of information concerning pending or anticipated judicial proceedings.

7. If an act of delinquency is publicized, news media should be informed of the disposition of the case.

Again we see an approval of withholding of news by the judge—"at his discretion" names may be released.

Such are the recommendations to the judges and to the members of the fourth estate, released in April, 1965. The sponsors are students of the problem, most of them with a wealth of practical experience. Whether, after ten or twenty years have passed, the best judgment of a similar group will be the same, only time can tell. There are constant changes in the philosophy and practical approach of educators in their field and social workers in theirs. Pediatricians run through phases—four hour feedings, three hour, two hour, whenever the baby is hungry like nature intended, and then, *presto*, back to four hours. Similarly, the results of overmuch secrecy and protection against publicity (a natural concomitant of crime) may impel the resurgence of the belief that adverse publicity deters crime, and does not encourage exhibitionists as some now say.

Obviously, the quoted recommendations do not have force of law and are not binding except as, coincidentally, one parallels the statutes or local rules. Newsmen should find them helpful (i) in showing star-chamber-minded judges the error of their ways, and (ii) in deciding what news of juvenile misbehavior and punishment is in the public interest. Certainly the tragedies of children haled into juvenile court should not be exploited for sake of circulation or Nielsen ratings. Equally certain is the fundamental that there are occasions when the facts should be told and the participants identified regardless of the current recommendations of workers in that vineyard or the preferences of a judge—unless of course the publication is contrary to law or would generate a contempt of court.

Subject to statutory restrictions in respect to publishing stories concerning the perpetration of offenses by youth, there is a wide scope for editorial discretion. In a large city it may be deemed useless or even harmful to publish names as a matter of course. In a nearby town, news media may be convinced that, with occasional exceptions, it is a public service to publish names. Depending on the local situation and tradition and the personalities involved, the geography may be reversed. In the smaller community it may be thought best not to let the neighbors know more than they learn by word of mouth, and in the city the publicity may be deemed an instrument of law enforcement. And in either area a wave of juvenile delinquency may change what was once deemed a firm opinion.

Implicit in the quoted report is the recognition that, as stated by John Henry Wigmore in his description of the modern juvenile court:

> Privacy of examination of the delinquent and his family is . . . regarded as generally useful and occasionally essential; and the statutes usually provide for this.
> But insofar as . . . practice habitually exercises the power [of strict privacy], it has its [risks]. No court of justice can afford habitually to conduct its proceedings strictly in private.

Again, a great scholar of the law implicitly recognizes media as a handmaiden of justice, "an indispensable element," as phrased by Mr. Justice Frankfurter.

Since many who believe in minimum reporting of juvenile court proceedings would, in effect, ultimately put control of the news to be released (not direction as to what should be published*) in the hands of the judge, the operative result of their philosophy would be a secrecy inconsistent with public surveillance of the workings of an important branch of the judicial system.

---

* Some zealots seem to favor giving the judge supervisory discretion over what may be printed.

However, the specter of an occasional star chamber, dominated by a judge unsuited to his assignment, must not distort the day-to-day picture. Most of the judges presiding in juvenile court are dedicated to their baffling task. They will recognize news as a necessary adjunct to the judicial machinery of a free society. They will cooperate with newsmen who show understanding of the over-all problem. When, in a particular situation, a difficult decision must be made, it should be made on the basis of public good.

CHAPTER 17

DANGER ZONES

*If a little knowledge is dangerous, where
is the man who has so much as to be out
of danger?*

T. H. HUXLEY

CHECK and double check. Usually any one of several men could
have corrected the error, or at least recognized the possible presence of defamation and referred the copy to someone for verification or scrutiny. When dealing with defamatory matter not
clearly privileged or easily· proved true, it is prudent: (i) to
double check the facts; (ii) to do so in such a fashion that every
juror will say, "The writer and, in fact, everyone handling the
copy did everything they could to be careful"; and (iii) when
proofreading and processing, to handle like an explosive.

CRIMES

Stories concerning crimes are apt to be libelous per se of
someone, if untrue. As cautioned in Part I of Chapter 7, until a
charge is filed, circumstances do not ordinarily warrant more
than a statement that the police are holding whomever it may

be for questioning in connection with the crime of which a story tells.

To say, "Blank was jailed on an open charge" may convey to the public the impression that a charge of some sort has been filed. "Blank was not charged but is being held," or "Blank is held in jail but has not been charged," is more accurate. Statements of this sort are justified because provably true. However, there are times when the nature of the crime or the prominence of those involved requires much bolder treatment. Under those circumstances, the responsibility of the source, the reputation of the accused, and all other factors must be weighed and a sound discretion exercised.

In any such story a denial of guilt should be as conspicuous as the accusation.

COLUMNISTS

Data are not available, but it is doubtless safe to assert that syndicated columns and columnists are involved in a disproportionate number of libel actions. A mathematician might say that the hazard of libel is in inverse relation to the distance. A column refers to someone resident in, say, Denver. As a practical matter, the story might be safe enough in any state other than Colorado, plus perhaps nearby areas of adjoining states. Before publication or broadcast a column should be read in the light of the local situation. If, despite the risk, a possibly libelous statement regarding local people is to be published, they should be given a chance to answer, preferably in the same issue, just as though the story had been written locally.

CRUSADES

A crusade series is vulnerable because the stories are not founded on spot news brought in through ordinary channels.

Crusade stories are unearthed by the reporter—the plaintiff claims maliciously. So crusade material should be viewed critically.

DOMESTIC DISCORD

Except when referring to persons with a history of domestic infelicity or to members of a set noted for the shifting of spouses, it should be assumed that a false statement of contemplated divorce or other assertion of critical domestic rift may be defamatory. In states where adultery is the only or principal ground for divorce, a false charge that Valerie was divorced by Henry may be libelous per se.

Where by statute or rule of court certain proceedings in a domestic relations court are supposed to be private in nature, there are two hazards—(i) want of the privilege which would be incident to the proceeding in open court, and (ii) contempt of court.

FINANCIAL NEWS AND COMMENT

Libel through disparagement of property is touched upon in Chapter 2. Sometimes financial writers and commentators not only disparage a business—they assert or intimate wrongful, perhaps fraudulent, conduct on the part of the corporate officers. There is no privilege when repeating the accusations and counteraccusations of a proxy fight, unless the latter is under the wing of right to reply (Chapter 9). As has been mentioned, cooperatives and charitable corporations, as well as corporations organized for profit, may be libeled. As in the case of columnists and commentators, the hazard of mistaken identity is not trivial.

JUVENILE DELINQUENTS

Reports and data concerning juvenile delinquents may not be public records. To protect the child, laws commonly authorize or require private hearings before the juvenile court. At his discretion, the judge may withhold a child's name. In such circumstances publication of a name obtained from juvenile court records or authorities may be wrongful—perhaps a contempt of court. When, however, a juvenile is formally charged in criminal court by indictment or information, there is no such restriction.

KNOW YOUR NUANCES

Chapter 2 mentions the meaning of words. If words are used precisely, there will be no opportunity for court or jury to construe language other than as intended. Is the following libel?

> The candidate for re-election is a shameless extrovert. Not only that, he practices nepotism. His only sister was once a thespian in Greenwich Village, New York. He matriculated with co-eds at the university. It is an established fact that before his marriage he habitually practiced celibacy.

The words "guilty" and "fined," for instance, refer to or at least connote a criminal procedure. Never use them when describing a civil action—in a civil action the court or jury finds for or against the defendant, and a judgment is entered.

NEW TRIALS, VERDICTS SET ASIDE, AND APPEALS

A lawsuit is not finally determined until (i) the time for an appeal has run without an appeal, or (ii) the court of final jurisdiction has spoken its final word. If the paper or newscaster has told of conviction of a crime or a finding of fraud or other obnoxious act in a civil case, a follow-up story should tell when:

(i) the verdict is set aside or a new trial granted by the trial court; or
(ii) the case has been reversed by the appellate court.

Otherwise a defendant (who may also resent the way the story of the trial was handled) may claim the paper did not publish a fair report of the entire proceedings.

CAUTION
Names of defendants appearing in dismissals of cases on appeal from police, traffic, and justice court convictions on motion of the prosecuting officer—thus vacating the conviction—should be checked to see if a story telling of the conviction was run. If it was, a story of the dismissal should be published. If it was not, the dismissal may be reported or ignored, depending on news value.

NO-NAME STORIES

There are two traps: (i) The person defamed may be identified despite the lack of name; or (ii) the no-name story may make difficult the use of the name in subsequent stories.

ILLUSTRATIONS
1. The headline says, "Suspect Grilled." The story says, "A clerk employed five years ago by County Treasurer Jones and dismissed last week by the present Treasurer is being questioned in connection with shortages in the pension fund." The clerk has been identified. If not a suspect but merely a helpful witness, he has been libeled.

2. A story recites "evidence" which, to the reader, convicts an unnamed man of murder. He is arrested and charged. The paper or newscaster reports the arrest by name, carefully refraining from tie-in to the anonymous story. But the suspect can show that some people knew him to be the man referred to in the first story.

The true murderer is found and confesses. The charge against the paper's suspect is dismissed. So is the reporter.

NAME NOT ENOUGH

The *London Express* remarked that "Harold Newstead, 30 year old Camberwell man who was jailed for nine months, liked having two wives at a time." In Camberwell there were two men of about that age named Harold Newstead. The one who had not been convicted of bigamy sued the publisher. *Query*: Does the story sufficiently segregate bigamist Harold Newstead from all other Harold Newsteads by describing him as the one who served a term? What if the name had been Jones or Smith with a common first name?

"NOT" WORDS

Like "not," a number of words make mistakes easy. "Not" may be typed or set as "now." Either makes sense when read and so is easily overlooked. "He is now in jail"—or "not," which is it? When the story defames, avoid prefixes and words vulnerable to error in transmittal and printing. When using telephone or telegraph or even writing "not guilty," there is more chance of the paper printing, or the newscaster saying, "guilty" than if the copy read "acquitted" or "innocent."

OBSCENITIES

Except as touched upon in the discussion of the unique status of a qualified political candidate, we have not discussed obscenities. There seemed no reason to do so. This book is not written for the edification of publishers of "girlie" magazines.

Briefest mention of the legal dilemma may be justified. The courts have not yet reached satisfactory and workable formulas to be used when determining:

    (i) whether the dominant theme (in words or pictures) appeals only to the prurient interest, or

   (ii) whether, viewed as a whole, there is a literary or artistic purpose.

These things must be gauged by contemporary standards of the community. Which community? Contemporary community standards in Pine Bluff, Arkansas (where they were recently in court on this very question), may differ from those of Hollywood. Can anyone delineate a national standard comprehending both Las Vegas and a New England village with Puritan traditions not forgotten?

Some groups favor widest latitude in publishing whatever one pleases—there must be no censorship—and they claim that federal and state constitutions are on their side. Others hold to stricter standards; they assert that they are on the side of the angels.

The end result is that each publication challenged in court must be decided pretty much on its own—another instance of balancing absolute freedom of communication with other desiderata. Again—as in case of right of privacy—there will be no problem as long as John Ruskin is remembered: One of his precepts was that good taste will answer moral problems. In the field of communications, it will answer most legal dilemmas.

RIVALRIES—REAL AND SIMULATED

For years Jack Benny and his good friend Fred Allen helped one another by throwing brickbats at each other. Their pattern is imitated, particularly on the air, by rival phone-in (shop-talk) programs, with sideswipes at newspaper columnists or reporters and the resulting tit-for-tat from those who use the printed page. Up to a point, this is good for all concerned—many in the audience enjoy a hearty brawl. Once it gets out of hand, participants are hurt. Suits are expectable, each subject to the several defenses available against men in the public eye who attack others.

PROMISES

There is a constant temptation to place too much reliance on promises that something will happen tomorrow—the report will be filed, the suspect will be named, the officer will be dismissed. These promises are not as góod as are the intentions of the men who make them because the situation may change overnight. Do not defame under the assumption that your evidence of truth will be born tomorrow. Never report a defamatory event in the past tense before that event has occurred.

Society

The society editor says such pleasant things that to her libel is almost a stranger—unless society includes a gossip column or commentator. The principal present hazard incident to the handling of social events is the expanding right of privacy cases predicated on approaching nudity in society pictures or too much prying into personal affairs, even though the words used sound friendly. See Chapter 13.

Sports

Sport pages and broadcasts cover more than high school and Ivy League contests. It is noticeable that since the rise of professional sports more libel cases than formerly originate in the sports room—insinuations that the goalie threw the game, or that a fighter was cowardly, are typical. Sport libel may be hard to defend; truth may be the only defense. His buddies may back the libeled player, even though before the publication they wished him off the team.

Libel suits have been brought and won by coaches, referees, race track officials, and other appendages.

What Law Governs?

The writing is published or the broadcast tower situated in state A. The publication circulates or the broadcast is heard or viewed also in states B, C, D, and E. Jones, a resident of one of the latter states, is defamed. If jurisdiction over the publisher or broadcaster is obtained in the plaintiff's state, its law may apply. Or, because the dissemination of the libel was in the plaintiff's state, its laws may govern even though suit is brought in some other state. If a story goes over the wires it may be published or broadcast in every state.

WIRE STORIES

A defamatory wire story purporting to be about a local person should not be published or broadcast unless it is checked locally to make sure as to identity and that the person named was at the place described in the story. Serious libel suits have been based upon wire stories telling of the participation of a local resident in an event occurring in a distant city when, as a matter of fact, the accused was safely at home. One wire story told of the arrest of a young woman in a "love nest" in San Francisco. It was passed along to an eager public in her home town, a thousand miles away, without being checked locally. The local girl could prove that instead of being in the love nest at the time of the arrest she had been attending church services presided over by her father, a bishop.

CHAPTER 18

COPYRIGHTS AND
LITERARY PROPERTY

> *The sweat of a man's brows, and the
> exudations of his brains, are as much a
> man's own property as the breeches upon
> his backside.*
>
> LAURENCE STERNE

COPYRIGHT grants the author of an original work or composition in literature or the arts, and his successors, the exclusive right to multiply copies for sale. Copyrights are issued under federal statute upon publication. The federal Constitution recognizes the needs and authorizes the Congress:

> To promote the progress of science and the useful arts by securing for limited times to authors . . . the exclusive right to their respective writings . . . [Art. 1, Sec. VIII].

Prior to publication the author may have enforceable common law rights of ownership.

OWNERSHIP WITHOUT COPYRIGHT

The Federal Copyright Act provides that it shall not be

construed to amend or limit the right of the author or proprietor of an unpublished work: (i) to prevent the copying, publication, or use thereof without his consent; and (ii) to recover damages if his rights be violated. Hence it is not safe to copy an uncopyrighted writing, drawing, picture, or other work unless: (i) with the provable consent of the creator or his successor as proprietor, or (ii) prior publication of the work is provable.

Within the law of defamation there may be a "publication" if the defamatory matter is communicated to one person (see p. 15). But it must not be assumed that a communication to one person or sometimes even to a considerable number of persons shifts the work into the public domain and makes it copyable with impunity. For example:

1. The reproduction of letters for profit is usually controlled by the writer-sender, not by the addressee. The latter may have no authority to release for publication. The author's right of privacy may also be involved. The principles of Chapter 13 would apply.
2. Delivering a manuscript for limited purposes (review, editing, or other) is not a publication.
3. The display of uncopyrighted pictures to groups is not necessarily a release into the public domain.
4. Theft of a manuscript does not terminate the rights of the lawful owner. The author of an uncopyrighted musical score would have protection even though a larcener had staged a nationwide broadcast.

Certain files of Senator Thomas J. Dodd were removed from his office at night, photocopied, and returned undamaged before the office resumed operations. Drew Pearson and Jack Anderson received copies of the documents, knowing of their unauthorized removal. They published excerpts, nationwide. Subject to possible review by the United States Supreme Court, the law of this important case is that Dodd may not recover damages under the theory that his literary property was stolen. The language of the Court of Appeals for the District of Columbia cannot be improved upon:

> . . . It has long been recognized that documents often have value above and beyond that springing from their physical possession. They may embody information or ideas whose economic value depends in part or in whole upon being kept secret. The question then arises whether the information taken by means of copying appellee's office files is of the type which the law of conversion protects.
>
> . . . The general rule has been that ideas or information are not subject to legal protection, but the law has developed exceptions to this rule. Where information is gathered and arranged at some cost and sold as a commodity on the market, it is properly protected as property. Where ideas are formulated with labor and inventive genius, as in the case of literary works or scientific researches, they are protected. Where they constitute instruments of fair and effective commercial competition, those who develop them may gather their fruits under the protection of the law.
>
> . . . The question here is not whether appellee had a right to keep his files from prying eyes, but whether the information taken from those files falls under the protection of the law of property, enforceable by a suit for conversion. In our view it does not. . . .
>
> . . . Insofar as we can tell, none of it amounts to literary property, to scientific invention, or to secret plans formulated by appellee for the conduct of commerce. Nor does it appear to be information held in any way for sale by appellee, analogous to the fresh news copy produced by a wire service.

The court also held that there was no invasion of Senator Dodd's right of privacy. In a footnote, the opinion states:

> A threshold question, not briefed by either party and

hence not decided by us, is the nature of the property right
held by appellee in the contents of the files in his Senate
office. Those files, themselves paid for by the United States,
are maintained in an office owned by the United States,
by employees of the United States. They are meant to con-
tribute to the work of appellee as an officer of the United
States. The question thus is not entirely free from doubt
whether appellee has title to the contents of the files or
has a right of exclusive possession of those contents, or is
a bailee, or even a mere custodian of those contents.

An authoritative court decision on this question in favor of an
unauthorized publisher would strengthen the position of media
in reporting on public affairs.

The caveat of the next paragraph is real but may be viewed
with a rule of reason. It has to do with quoting certain types
of speeches and lectures. Certainly, far more often than not,
the type of utterance reported by media invites publicity.
Consent to quote, as a whole or in part, is inherent in the public
nature of the occasion. Indeed, the speaker yearns for maximum
publicity. A fair report of what was said is safe.

Nevertheless, there may be a common law ownership of a
lecture on "Memory" or "Health through Hypnotism" or what
not. A lecture might be delivered as often as was "Acres of
Diamonds," yet not be surrendered into the public domain and
available for printing or broadcast.

The general rule is that when, with the permission of the
author or his successor, there is a general publication, the
common law protection afforded literary property is lost. Future
protection stems from adherence to the requirements of the
Federal Copyright Act. But there are exceptions. For example:
as between rival newsgathering and publishing agencies, current news has ownership aspects. Persistent copying of news
gathered by a competitor may amount to unfair competition.
But the "tip" that the event has occurred may be used by any-

one who makes an independent investigation and does his own composing.

BACKGROUND

The law of copyright of Western Europe can be traced back at least five hundred years. With Gutenberg the need grew.

Promptly in 1790, the Congress of the United States passed an act "for the encouragement of learning, by securing the copies of maps, charts and books to the authors and proprietors. . . ." Present law of copyright is found in (i) the Copyright Act of 1909, with some revisions; (ii) detailed rules and regulations issued under the act; and (iii) court decisions construing and enforcing the act and regulations.

Most principles applicable to literary property without copyright were developed by court decisions. In sharp contrast, copyright law is spelled out by federal statutes; the courts merely construe and enforce.

WHAT MAY BE COPYRIGHTED

A copyright is not a license to monopolize ideas and concepts. It does not give an exclusive right to report events or describe the sunset. Ordinary words and idioms as such are usable by all. Copyright has to do with phraseology, with the sequence of words and phrases, with the pictures used to express the idea, report the happening, tell the story, or advocate a cause—or with the sequence of notes used to create the tune or the rock and roll.

Copyrightable material includes nearly all original writings (except those issued by the federal government) and other things. Illustrations are:

> (i) books, periodicals, and newspapers, or portions thereof;

   (ii) lectures and sermons;

  (iii) musical compositions and plays;

  (iv) photographs, pictorial illustrations, drawings, and cartoons;

   (v) motion pictures and television shows;

  (vi) maps, drawings, and plastic works of a scientific or technical nature;

 (vii) works of art, models, designs for works of art, and a reproduction of a work of art.

The above inventory is not all-inclusive. The act says that its enumeration shall not be held to limit the subject matter. The listing of sermons would not exclude prayers.

So if there is a desire to copy material which is not clearly in the public domain and which might be subject to copyright, it is prudent to inquire of counsel—certainly if it carries a notice of copyright.

REGISTRATION

This chapter is not concerned with how to secure or sell or bequeath a copyright or how otherwise to deal with it as proprietor. The function here is to point out when there may be violations of the rights of the proprietor.

The procedures incident to registering a copyright (with the Library of Congress) are simple. The fees are nominal. But one should have a competent guide until the path is familiar.

DURATION—NOTICE

A copyright endures for twenty-eight years plus an extension of twenty-eight years if the author makes timely application for renewal in accordance with the act. This right to renew passes to the successors of a deceased author as defined in the act. A work first published, say, forty years ago may or may not be protected by copyright. There have been statutory extensions which must be specifically checked in any borderline situation.

On most printed matter the minimum required notice consists of "Copyright," "Copr.," or the symbol © accompanied by the name of the proprietor and the year in which the copyright was secured. The symbol © accompanied by the initials, monogram, mark, or symbol of the proprietor puts one on notice that there may be sufficient identification elsewhere on the copy; or on its back, permanent base, or pedestal; or on the substance on which the copy is mounted.

A decision that a notice is insufficient and that the work is in the public domain should never be made without advice of counsel.

REVIEWS AND CRITICISM

A copyrighted work is subject to fair criticism, favorable or unfavorable, serious or humorous. To that end it may be quoted and it may be described by words or pictures. But the quotations must not be of such length or the quotations and pictures so numerous that public demand to read or view the copyrighted work will be materially reduced.

The borderline between a proper review and excessive quotations (or pictures) cannot be fixed in advance by formulas applicable to all situations. If the review of the work is honestly and capably written as such, it is unlikely that either quotations or pictures will exceed permitted limits.

While criticism may be severe, the reviewer does not usually enjoy the latitude afforded critics of public affairs. See Chapter 8, "Comment and Criticism," particularly pages 77 and 82. Later we will notice other aspects of fair use.

INFRINGEMENTS

The comments and illustrations of this and the following two sections in respect to infringements apply alike to violations of common law rights of ownership before publication and infringement of a statutory copyright.

It is easy to state a general rule: any unfair appropriation of the results of the imagination, skill, and labors of the original author will constitute an offense. If the whole or a substantial part is plagiarized in the words of the original, the infringement is plain. So, too, if there is a persistent pattern of paraphrasing or variation without adequate justification. But mere similarity is not always enough. Suppose two scholars are independently engaged in historical research in a narrow field. They examine the same original documents; they read and quote many of the same old books and manuscripts. Their writings may be much the same, page after page. Yet neither has used the work of the other. Or assume that two skilled reporters cover the same event. Their stories may be very similar, though composed independently.

Another way to phrase the test is whether the one charged with the infringement has produced independently or has unfairly cribbed the product of the author.

Whether there has been a violation of the rights of the proprietor depends upon the facts of and circumstances surrounding each disputed case. A choral instructor incorporated a copyrighted song in a new arrangement and had his chorus sing it. The court found an infringement. In another decision, rearrangement of a copyrighted hymn for the church choir was held a fair use. In still another case, the church itself was held liable when the choir-director–organist infringed a copyright of music.

When applying these principles, one must remember that the author will not be protected in his ideas, his theories; he will be protected in his manner of expressing them—his rhetoric and the illustrations he uses. A cartographer may copyright his map of an island; it may not be copied with impunity. Another cartographer may survey that island and produce a map almost identical; his is an independent work.

EXAMPLES OF INFRINGEMENTS

The comparison of writings, music, and other works to ascertain if there has been an infringement is often a long process. Indeed, one in-depth analysis might well consume more pages than this entire chapter. Below are listed a number of situations which resulted in a court decision to the effect that there had been an infringement. They are merely markers to indicate typical danger areas.

1. An unauthorized abridgment or rearrangement of copyrighted articles from a newspaper or magazine may be a violation. (The creation of an index may be a new work.)
2. The draftsman of an insurance policy or other legal document has no monopoly on the thought which the language expresses. But in flagrant situations of plagiarism there may be a violation.
3. Copyrighted advertising may not be used or copied.
4. The proprietor of a copyright for a musical composition has rights beyond his exclusive right to print—including a public performance for profit. Broadcasting is a public performance.
5. A member of an audience may take extensive notes and use the knowledge he has gained in his own affairs. But, without consent, he may not print and distribute or orally deliver a lecture (or other speech not in the public domain) without the author's consent.
6. A writer of plays has wide protection but (to repeat) he cannot pre-empt exclusive control of a field of thought on a particular subject or theme.
7. Vice Admiral Rickover prepared speeches on his own time, not as a part of his official duties. He delivered them to private organizations. They had been repro-

duced by government facilities for purposes of security clearance and publicity. The speeches were his private property, and he was entitled to a copyright.

8. As applied to a pattern for fabrics—"graphic plagiarism" occurs when the copyist preserves the structure and important characteristics of the original design, notwithstanding systematic variation of each subordinate detail.

The similarity must be recognizable by ordinary observation. Experts may be called as witnesses. But the test is not whether hypercritical dissection reveals seeming similarities—particularly when writings are about the same event or person or subject, theory or theme. The occurrence of the same errors in two different writings is one of the most persuasive proofs of copying.

FAIR USE

An illustrative list of decisions which held there was *not* a violation (some of them "near miss" situations!) might be compiled. That would be a disservice. It might trap someone into publishing material which, under slightly changed circumstances, the court would hold to be protected.

Reviews and criticisms, already discussed, are facets of fair use. Fair use is the privilege of persons other than the copyright owner to use the material in a reasonable manner without his consent.

The doctrine of fair use is most often applied when scientific, legal, and historical materials are involved and also in connection with compilations, maps, listings, digests, and other works designed to inform. The purpose for which the use is made is of major importance. If the challenged use is for the advancement of science or the arts or knowledge generally it might well be a fair use although the same *quantum* of use for commercial purposes would be an undeniable infringement. If in doubt, secure consent; almost always it is granted readily.

As has already been indicated in another framework, a copyrighted story of a news event, published in the morning paper, may not be copied. The happening of that event, however, is a fact. The afternoon paper may send out its photographers and newsmen and create a story of its own.

LIABILITY FOR VIOLATIONS

Corporations and participating individuals are liable just about as they would be in suits based on defamation or violation of privacy. A television company is chargeable with the conduct of staff members employed to produce a broadcast script. The manager of a radio station may be personally liable just as is the editor of a newspaper. The vendor of an infringing work may be liable. So may the owner of a store who permits a concessionaire to violate copyrights. A person who employs an orchestra may be in a similar situation.

INTERNATIONAL EFFECT

Copyright laws do not have extraterritorial efficacy. However there are international conventions extending the rights that will be protected by copyright. The Berne Convention of 1886 and the Unesco Universal Copyright Convention of 1952 (effective in the United States in 1955) are the most notable. It must not be assumed that because the material was published or printed abroad it is copyable.

ACTIONABLE INFRINGEMENTS

He who claims to be the owner of the copyright cannot recover damages for a violation or stop further publication by the alleged infringer unless: (i) there has been a sufficient compliance with the provisions of the act in respect to registration, and (ii) what he registered was copyrightable. No copyright will protect the reproduction of material already in the public domain. When the requirements of registration have been met, lack of intention to infringe is usually not a defense. See the discussion of "intention" in respect to defamation (pp. 13, 15, 28-35).

The plaintiff does not have to demonstrate that the author, artist, or composer was a genius; the copyrighted material need not be strikingly unique or novel. All that is required is that the creator has done something on his own which is more than a variation.

DAMAGES—CRIMINAL SANCTIONS

It is a misdemeanor willfully and for profit to infringe a copyright or knowingly to aid or abet such infringement.

Even though innocent of wrongful intent, the purloiner of another's literary property before registration or of his copyrighted property after valid registration may be required to pay damages to the owner.

TRADEMARKS

A trademark is an identification—by sign, symbol, picture, pictograph, or letters—by which the articles produced or dealt in by a particular person or organization may be distinguished from those produced or dealt in by others. The products, the articles, may be manufactured and sold by others.

The laws of many states provide for the registration of trademarks. Federal laws provide for registration of trademarks used in interstate or foreign commerce.

Copyrights, patents, and trademarks have a common element. They all stem from legal recognition of property rights derived from creative ability (of an inventor, writer, artist, composer) or from quality in performance—a good product, year after year. Day after day the literary production of a columnist could be copyrighted. If he regularly uses a certain distinctive headline, that may be registered as a trademark.

As noted in illustrations already given, a label with at least a modicum of artistic merit and ingenuity may be copyrighted. Within it or within an advertisement may be a trademark— registered as such and also used separately.

Like copyrights, patents are not of indefinite duration. If a man ingeniously makes a grandfather's clock, he and his successors will own it forever. But if he invents a device to make all clocks better, he and his successors will own the invention no longer than the statutory period.

CHAPTER 19

THIRTY

The great end of life is not knowledge but action.

T. H. HUXLEY

NATURAL questions are: In the field of communications is the law becoming more or less strict? Are shackles being put upon the wrists of publishers? Looking only to fundamentals, there are two answers. At first glance they seem inconsistent, but actually they are not.

When performing the vital functions of scrutinizing, reporting, and commenting upon public affairs, media are afforded greater protection than was formerly available to shield them.

When publicizing purely personal and private affairs, media are now held to higher standards of accuracy and consideration than in years past. The extension of protection to persons not in the public eye flows through the channel of the right of privacy.

The strengthening of safeguards when reporting or commenting upon matters of public concern is not inconsistent with the increasing strictness of the courts in respect to assuring fair trials, as recounted in Chapter 16 and Part II of Chapter 12 where courtroom photography is discussed.

We have but described the high spots—perhaps not all of them. Nevertheless, study and periodic reading of the rules here given will enable anyone dealing with writings, pictures, or broadcasting to recognize the danger signals.

Possible libel having been recognized, a story or editorial satisfactory to all but the most ardent propagandist can be produced without appreciable risk (or, at least, without undue risk) in almost every situation.

Like a chart, this book notes the rocks and shallows and shows the aids to navigation. Vast areas of clear sailing are unmentioned. There is plenty of room to maneuver stories and editorials and to publish and broadcast pictures if a wary eye is kept on the markers here listed. As emphasized in Chapter 1, because this is a danger signal manual, *in close cases the law has been stated in stricter terms than the court should enforce.* Sometimes exceptions to and variations of the rules here given will be sufficient legal answer if a publication or broadcast is questioned in court. But to go into them in this book would be a disservice to the men and women for whom it is written.

Often it is difficult to defend a libel suit. Just as often it is difficult for the plaintiff to win—particularly when the plaintiff's past is shady and it is clear that the publisher or broadcaster was careful and the mistake natural, hence perhaps excusable. Jurymen, too, have erasers on their pencils.

Most rules of law are subject to exceptions. This is especially so in the field of libel. There the law must permit actual injury to be done without redress; novel and involved principles are brought into play. There has been no attempt to write a legal treatise, suitable for use by lawyers or a judge. Because every month brings fresh decisions from the court, a book purporting to delve into every detail would be outmoded before it was off the press.

The objective here has been to state the basic rules in simple terms and to show how they apply to typical situations. Except when the preceding pages have given express or implicit warning of the hazards of local idiosyncrasies, these fundamental principles and concepts should be adequate guideposts.

If, by inviting closer collaboration with counsel, we have persuaded the publisher to seek advice in advance, we shall have made a great contribution to pocketbooks as well as to peace of mind. An attorney is inexpensive when consulted in advance, relatively costly when called in after the event. One of the purposes of this book is to promote a sixth sense as to when counsel should be called.

THE RIGHT TO KNOW

Because freedom of the press is taken for granted in this country, it is easy to forget that (i) the right is relatively new; (ii) in many lands it does not exist; and (iii) there are forces which would undermine it here. An eminent American historian remarked, "We need, from time to time, to take a look at the things that go without saying to see if they are still going."

Freedom of the press and freedom of speech were written into the federal Constitution at a time when there were no such freedoms in England. Two decades after the adoption of our Constitution, an English publisher was convicted of crime because he criticized Parliament.

As was stated in the introduction and as, we hope, is implicit throughout, the purpose of this manual is not to frighten publishers and broadcasters into saying less. It is to help them be secure in saying what should be said. Many a bureaucrat, in Washington, in state capitals, in the city hall, and in the county courthouse, would prefer that the news touching governmental affairs be limited to mimeographed handouts. The premise of this book is that, except where national security is actually involved, the citizens of this country have a right to know what is going on. Unless they do, the country will not long remain free.

Early in the book it was mentioned that, when used here, the words "publisher," "publish," and "publishing" are words of art referring to the communication of the defamation, however, communicated. They include the writer of a letter as well as all persons involved in the production, printing, and (possibly) circulation of a newspaper, magazine, book, or circular. They include cameramen, processors, commentators, and everyone who participates in putting the defamatory broadcast on the air, as well as the owner of the station. They include the person who displays a statue as well as the sculptor and the institution which exhibits a defamatory picture as well as the artist.

In short—all those who communicate in any fashion are included. Their messages can be fully as effective, arouse fewer antagonisms, and be more profitable if said safely.

INDEX

Ad-lib, 6, 28, 63, 83, 157
Advertisements, 34-35, 38-42 *passim*, 66, 131
  Political, 38-39, 41, 63
  Right of privacy, 113
American Bar Association, 146
American Society of Newspaper Editors, 137-38
Appeals, 154-55

Bill of Rights, 9, 93, 133
Black, Hugo L., 81
Books, 6-7, 119 and *passim*
Boston Bar Association, 140-42
Brandeis, Louis D., 107
"Broadcast," defined, 15-16
Broadcasts. *See* Political broadcasts; Radio; Television

California Supreme Court, 45
Carelessness, 33-34
Cartoons and sketches, 15, 96, 101
Chicago Tribune, 31
Coined names, 32
Colliers magazine, 89
Columnists, 85, 152, 153
Comment and criticism, 6, 48, 76-85, 87, 94

Comment and criticism—*Cont.*
  Concerning
    Candidates, 79
    Commentators, 85
    Courts and judges, 80-81, 95
    Events of public concern, 80
    Government, 83
    Private ventures, 80
    Public officials, 77-79, 82
    Sundry public individuals, 82
  Distinguished from privilege, 76-77
  Multiple critiques, 84
  Who may be criticized, 77
Communications Act, 40, 116, 119, 122, 125
Confessions, 56, 135, 136, 141, 144-45
Conflict between freedom of the press and fair trial, 94, 133-50
  Guidelines, 135, 138, 139, 140-41, 142
Consent. *See* Defense
Contempt of court, 93-98, 105, 120, 134, 143, 153, 154
  Case concluded, 97
  Criticism of court, 80-81
  Defined, 95
  Fair trial, 93-94, 102

INDEX

Contempt of court—*Cont.*
  Photography, 99, 102
  Truth not defense, 98
  Typical contempts, 95-96
  Writer's refusal to testify, 96
Copyrights, 160, 164-71
  Background, 164
  Constitutional provisions, 160
  Damages, 171
  Duration, 165
  Fair use, 169
  Infringements, 168, 170
  International effect, 170
  Liability, 170
  Registration, 165
  Reviews and criticism, 166
  Trademarks, 171-72
  What may be copyrighted, 164
Correction and retraction, 35, 90-92
Crime stories, 151-52
Criticism. *See* Comment and criticism
Crusade series, 152-53

Damages, 7, 18, 34
Defamation, 10 and *passim*
Defenses, 11, 18, 25, 29, 34, 37, 50, 64, 79, 83, 84, 121
  Consent, 87-88, 108
  Contempt, 98
  Privilege, 47
  Pseudo consent, 88
  Retraction, 90-91
  Right of privacy, 113-14
  Truth, 86-87, 92, 98, 113-14
Departure from script. *See* Ad-lib
Disc jockey. *See* Ad-lib
Disparagement of property, 12-13, 38
Domestic discord, 153

England, 4, 48-49, 81-82, 145, 175
Estes, Billie Sol, case (1965), 103-5

"Fairness doctrine," 119-21, 122, 127, 130
Fair trial, 93, 94, 95, 102, 103, 134-37, 138-50, 173-74
  See also Conflict between freedom of press and fair trial
Faubus, Orval E., 61
Federal Communications Commission, 6, 69, 116, 119, 122-23, 125, 126, 129, 130, 132
  See also Political broadcasts
Financial news, 153
France, 4, 145
Francis, John J., 136-37
Frankfurter, Felix, 81, 149
Freedom of the press, 93, 94, 95, 96, 137-39, 140-50, 175
  See also Conflict between freedom of press and fair trial

Group libel, 33

Harlan, John M., 104
Harriman, Averill, 61
Headlines, 29-30
Hearsay, 13-14

Identification, 30-32, 37, 71-72, 99-101, 135, 155-56
Innocent dissemination, 16
Intention, 13, 15, 28-35
Interpretation of words, 14-15
Iowa Supreme Court, 84

Jurisdiction, 115, 118, 158-59
Juvenile problems, 96, 111, 141, 145-50, 153-54

Kansas Supreme Court, 70
Kentucky Supreme Court, 108

Libel
    Civil, types of, 11-13
    Criminal, 14
    Defined, 3, 10-14
    History, 4-5
    Opinion, 12
    Seditious, 14
    Types, 29-35
    See also Libel law; Libel per se
Libel law, 48-49, 65, 94, 134, 174-75
    See also Libel; Libel per se
Libel per se, 13, 15, 18-27 passim, 28, 40, 60, 64, 66, 68, 70, 87, 100, 101, 113, 117, 151, 153
    Specific words and phrases, 19-25
    Types, 26
    See also Libel; Libel law
Literary Property, 160-64
    Dodd case, 161-63
    Lectures, 163
    News, 163
    Owner's rights, 161
    Violations, 161
Los Angeles Examiner, 110

Magazines, 6-7, 16, 41, 119 and passim
Malice, 33-34, 39, 66, 71, 79, 82, 85, 86, 90, 92, 113
Massachusetts Bar Association, 140-42
Massachusetts Newspaper Information Service, 140-42
"Media," defined, 15-16
Minneapolis Tribune, 89
Mistake. See Identification; Intention; Negligent mistake
Montague, Lady Mary Wortley, 4
Motion pictures, 101. See also Photography

National Broadcasting Company, 13, 110
National Council on Crimes and Delinquency, 146-48
Negligent mistake, 34-35
New Jersey Supreme Court, 135-37
New Mexico Supreme Court, 45
Newspapers, 4-5, 5-6, 16, 29-30, 41, 119 and passim
News services. See Wire services
New trial, verdict set aside, 154-55
New York Court of Appeals, 112
New York Daily News, 67, 70
New Yorker, 110
New York Times, 39
New York Times case (1964), 39, 63, 65, 66, 67, 70, 71, 74, 77, 78, 79, 80
No-name stories, 155
"Not" words, 156

Obscenities, 127, 156-57
Oregon Association of Broadcasters, 142-43
Oregon Bar Association, 142-43
Oregon Newspaper Publishers Association, 142-43

Penalty, 7, 18, 34
Pennsylvania Supreme Court, 61
Photography, 94, 96, 99-106, 111
    In courtroom, 102-6
Police, 55-56, 62, 136, 141
Political broadcasts, 122-32
    By candidates, 122-29
    By noncandidates, 129-31
    Candidate libeled, 130-32
    Censorship, 126-27
    Equal opportunity, 128
    Obscenity, 127
    "Use," 125-26
    See also Advertisements; Com-

Political broadcasts—*Cont.*
   munications Act; Political
   candidates, legally qualified
Political candidates, legally quali-
   fied, 118, 120, 123
Privacy. *See* Right of privacy
Privilege, absolute, 43-47 *passim*,
   75, 139
  Administrative, 46, 59
  Government, 44-46
  Judicial, 44
  Legislative, 44
Privilege, qualified or conditional,
   36-40 *passim*, 43, 47-75 *pas-*
   sim, 76, 79, 80, 83, 84, 87, 88,
   90, 94, 99, 139, 143, 153
  Abuse of privilege, 72
  Calculated risk, 73-75, 77, 143
  Definition, 47
  Identifying privilege, 71-72
  Loss of privilege, 70-71
  Occasions of privilege
    Abatement proceedings, 52
    Administrative hearings, 57
    Church proceedings, 69
    City or town council, 57
    Community clubs, 69
    Complaints, contents of, 52
    Congress, 57
    Conventions, 69
    Coroner's jury, 53-54
    Court proceedings, 50-53
    Depositions, 56
    Ecclesiastical trials, 69
    Executive and administrative
     proceedings, 58-60
    Ex parte hearings, 51
    Grand jury, 54
    Hearings and investigations,
     57
    Indictments, 55
    Informations, 55
    Judicial proceedings, 50-56

Privilege—*Cont.*
    Legislative proceedings, 56-58
    Lodge proceedings, 69
    Pleadings, contents of, 52
    Police news, 55-56
    Political gatherings, 69
    Public officers, 60-63, 66
     As candidates, 63
    Recall petitions, 68
    Replies to attacks, 68-69
    School board, 57
    Semipublic proceedings, 69
    Statements stricken from rec-
     ord, 51
    Stockholders' meetings, 69
    Warrant for arrest, 55
  Weak privilege, 72-73
Punitive damages. *See* Damages
"Publisher," defined, 15-16

Quotations, 36-37
  Officeholders as candidates, 63
  Public statements by officials, 60-
   63

Radio, 5, 6, 16, 41, 64, 83, 102, 103,
   116-21, 122-32 and *passim*
  Due care, 117-18
  Network programs, 118
  What law applies, 118, 158-59
  See also "Fairness doctrine"; Po-
   litical broadcasts
Replies to attack, 88-89
Retraction. *See* Correction and re-
   traction
Right of privacy, 80, 94, 105, 106,
   107-15, 120, 129-30, 134, 173
  Advertisements, 113
  Commercial use, 113
  Deceased persons, 114
  Good taste, 109
  History, 107-8

Right of Privacy—*Cont.*
Inapplicable to
Consent, 108
News, 108-9
Privileged communication, 109
Prominent subject, 109, 158
Public event of great impor-
tance, 109
Pictures, 99, 101, 110-11, 158
Public events, 112-13
Stale news, 110
Truth not defense, 113-14

Saturday Evening Post, 114
Scranton *Times,* 61
Society news, 158
Sports news, 158
Successive stories, 33

Television, 5, 6, 16, 41, 64, 83, 94,
101-2, 111, 112, 116-21, 122-
32 and *passim*
Criminal trials, 103-5
Due care, 117-18
Network programs, 118
What law applies, 118, 158-59

Television—*Cont.*
See also "Fairness doctrine"; Po-
litical broadcasts
Truth. *See* Defenses

United States Constitution, 66, 78,
79, 93, 133, 175
United States Court of Appeals, 67,
114, 126
United States Department of Justice, 134-35
United States Post Office, 16-17,
38, 41-42
United States Supreme Court, 39,
65, 81, 103, 104, 140
Utah Supreme Court, 46

Warren, Earl, 104
Warren Commission, 59
Washington Supreme Court, 47
Wenatchee Daily World, 146
West Virginia Supreme Court, 65
Wigmore, John Henry, 149
Wire services, 30, 36, 159
Words. *See* Interpretation of words